THE
ROYAL HOUSE
OF
GREECE

THE
ROYAL HOUSE
OF
GREECE

PRINCE MICHAEL OF GREECE
ALAN PALMER

WEIDENFELD AND NICOLSON
LONDON

The Publishers wish hereby to express their gratitude to Alexander P. Papamarkou, without whose assistance this book would not have seen the light of day.

First published in Great Britain in 1990 by
George Weidenfeld and Nicolson Ltd,
91 Clapham High Street, London SW4 7TA

British Library Cataloguing in Publication Data
Michael, *Prince of Greece*
The Royal House of Greece
1. Greece. Royal families, history
I. Title II. Palmer, Alan *1926–*
949.500922

ISBN 0–297–83060–0

Designed by Benn Linfield

Printed in Great Britain by
Butler & Tanner Ltd, Frome and London

Half-title: The Acropolis of Athens in the early years of George I's reign, before the modern city encroached upon the glories of the past.

Frontispiece: A royal family gathering in Denmark, 1896. George I (second from left) stands with his sisters the Dowager Empress Marie Feodorovna and the Princess of Wales. Their mother, Queen Louise is in a wheelchair. The future King George V of Great Britain (far right) sits with his sister Victoria and his wife (Queen Mary). At her feet is Prince Christian of Denmark, who later became King Christian X.

CONTENTS

FOREWORD

by HRH Prince Michael of Greece

The Greek royal family is the fruit of an unlikely union, a union between the descendants of Vikings with those of Antiquity and Byzantium. Yet, as frequently occurs in such odd alliances, the result has been, and still remains, a happy one. Although we did not start in Greece we belong to Greece. Unless one speaks with racial bias, Greekness does not imply membership to an ethnic group. On the contrary, it always used to mean (and, I like to think, still does mean) partaking in a certain spiritual outlook, religion and language; sharing a common body of knowledge and an appreciation of a way of life.

And my forebears, my relatives, possessed an inalienable right to their nationality. Side by side with their people, they endured two world conflicts, at least three struggles for national liberation, and a full-blown civil war; not to mention a long series of crises, perils and periods of acute suffering. Four times they were deposed and dispossessed; their lives were often lived in exile. On the other hand, in the long term, they successfully doubled Greece's land area, and more often than I can count, have helped the country back on its feet when the Greeks were reeling from the blows of fortune.

Above all, they loved Greece. They never asked for, nor expected, a reward for their service. They took nothing. They worked for the nation's greater good, laboured on its behalf, sacrificed themselves for it; not out of heroism, or a sense of obligation, but simply because they loved their country. For glory they cared less than nothing. What did it matter if there were no statues, no mention of them in the schoolbooks? It was always enough for them that they had been happy, very happy, in Greece, despite the trials they had to endure.

As I write this, I seem to see a procession from my family's past; the shades of men and women whom I never saw, but whom I know intimately from stories told and retold. First, my grandfather George I, who left his homeland and his family at the age of eighteen, to follow an uncertain destiny – yet in the end, established an absolute record for political longevity in Greece, by reigning there for half a century. Next I see

Four generations of kings: Christian IX of Denmark holds his great-grandson, the future George II; George I (left); Crown Prince Constantine (right).

An engraving of Athens, with Mount Lycabettos in the background, at the start of George I's reign in 1863. The palace was built for King Otho of Greece and financed by his father King Louis I of Bavaria.

the gentle Queen Olga, kindliness personified, utterly disarming; and Constantine I, who won Greece's provinces by the sword, only to meet the wretched fate of all our country's greatest men, who are first adored, then violently attacked.

Then came Queen Sophie, putting the best face on terrible adversity, gallantly concealing her anguish at the death of her son Alexander, a romantic victim who was struck down in his prime. Then the shy, dutiful George II, who was deeply respected by all who knew him, including his bitterest opponents. And then my uncles and my father, all in uniform: George, Nicholas, André, Christopher. Patriots to a man, great-hearted and erudite, they were always more at ease amid simple surroundings: they shared with all Greeks a taste for frankness and warm humanity, qualities they reflected in their own large natures. I can still hear their laughter today, for theirs was a humour that was irrepressible.

And then my cousins – Helene, Cécile, Marina, Tiny – these in particular among others. They were the 'lovely Greek Princesses', beautiful, elegant women who turned all heads wherever they went.

Last of all came the figures I myself knew most intimately: Paul I and Queen Frederica, who worked tirelessly to heal the scars of a tragic civil war, then presided over the nation's rebirth, always taking care of the needy. May I be allowed to mention personal experience in order to evoke them. As a teenager, I was sent to live with my relatives, whom I scarcely knew at all. Like any other Greek, I wondered what sort of people they might be, this family living in the wooded hills of Tatoi. I discovered that father, mother and the three children were all totally preoccupied with a single idea, which was Greece. Yet at the same time, they were warm-hearted and utterly generous, hospitable and cheerful individuals in a united, loving family. Since that time, the years have taken their toll: there have been deaths as well as births. But nothing has happened to change my first impression.

What of the future? I can only note that the last five thousand years in Greek history have largely consisted of events that nobody expected. Today, as in the past, anything could happen.

I am glad to have been so closely involved with the making of this book published on the occasion of the Fiftieth Birthday of His Majesty King Constantine II.

King Christian IX of Denmark (1838–1906), father of George I. He was recognized as heir-presumptive to the childless Frederick VII by the Danish Succession Law of 1853, acceding in November 1863, five months after his son became King of the Hellenes.

I

—

DEMOCRACY UNDER A KING

On an April morning in 1863 a Danish naval cadet left his Copenhagen home and turned down the Amaliegade towards the waterfront, along the Langelinie. He was a tall, thin young man, light-haired and clean shaven, with blue eyes and a stubborn chin and, as usual, he carried with him a packet of sandwiches for lunch. 'One of the sandwiches had sardines in it', he told his son several years later, 'and it was wrapped in an extra piece of newspaper to prevent the oil from leaking out. I glanced at the paper and read to my delighted amazement that I was King of the Hellenes.' It was a strange way for a seventeen-year-old prince to discover the destiny awaiting him.

Prince William of Denmark – Christian William Ferdinand Adolf George of Schleswig-Holstein-Sonderburg-Glucksburg, to accord the prince the full resonance of his titles – was born in Copenhagen on Christmas Eve, 1845. At that time his father, Prince Christian, was a cavalry Guards officer, outside the direct line of succession to the Danish throne, but the absence of male heirs in the immediate royal family led, six years later, to his recognition as heir presumptive. Soon afterwards he received as his official residence Bernstorff Castle, an eighteenth-century château five miles north of central Copenhagen set in fine parkland which looked out towards the Sound and the Swedish coast; and there Prince William spent much of a boyhood which he shared with an elder brother, Frederick, and a tomboy sister, Alexandra, almost exactly a year his senior. A second sister, Dagmar, was two years younger than William. He was nearly eight when his third sister, Thyra, was born and almost thirteen before he had another brother, Waldemar.

Life at Bernstorff was relaxed and socially democratic, and a similar informality prevailed in the family's town house, the so-called 'Yellow Palace', a few hundred yards from the King's residence, the Amalienborg. Prince William and his sisters were accustomed to wandering freely around the countryside, greeting villagers and townsfolk and, so far as they could, sharing with them the bonds of a simple humanity. William, a lively boy who enjoyed practical jokes, became an accomplished horseman but, like so many of his countrymen, he responded readily to the call of the high seas. As a youngster of fifteen he experienced the rigours of a voyage to Iceland and it was assumed that, although Prince Christian was a soldier, his second son would follow a career in the Danish navy. Then suddenly, in the spring of 1862, he became aware of the high status which his father's family now enjoyed in Europe, for there was talk of a fine marriage which would carry his favourite companion, Princess Alexandra, either into the imperial dynasty of Russia or the British royal family. At last, in mid-September, her engagement to the Prince of Wales was made public. On the first Saturday in March Prince William was among the family group who followed his sister ashore at Gravesend to witness the most enthusiastic welcome ever given by an English crowd to a royal bride 'from over the sea'. After delighting in such uninhibited enthusiasm – and with a written naval examination gloomily imminent – Prince William returned to Copenhagen 'hoping', as he recalled to his son, 'that something exciting would happen'. And there before him one morning came that extraordinary newspaper report: an assembly in Athens, 1,500 miles away, had voted in favour of his accession as sovereign ruler of the peoples of Hellas.

Prince William was, however, still legally under age. Would he be allowed to accept the crown? King Frederick VII of Denmark had no doubts: the Greek offer was a compliment to the Danish royal house; in his opinion, to refuse the crown of the Hellenes would be unthinkable. But neither Prince Christian nor his consort, Princess Louise, was so sanguine. By 1863 Greece had been a kingdom for a third of a century, her independence formally guaranteed by three Protecting Powers – Great Britain, France and Russia. After several rebuffs, these Protecting Powers had, in October 1832, successfully induced Prince Otto of Bavaria to become King Otho, the first crowned sovereign of Greece. This difficult role, made harder by occasional intimidation from his British and French Protectors, was one which the childless King Otho sought to fulfil with muddle-headed conscientiousness until an insurrection in October 1862 forced him and his Queen, Amalia, to flee the country aboard a British warship and return to Munich. Prince Christian – who was a very distant kinsman of Queen Amalia – was uneasy: Otho, he pointed out, had never abdicated and was therefore still titular King of Greece; and the Greek people themselves had originally voted overwhelmingly not for a Dane, but for Queen Victoria's second son, Prince Alfred, Duke of Edinburgh. He recognized that the Duke was ineligible, since the three Protectors had imposed a self-denying ordinance on members of their own royal families, but if Prince William were to become king his father sought guarantees safeguarding the young man's titles and income. He also encouraged the British Prime Minister, Palmerston, to persist with an earlier proposal that, in accepting a new king of whom Britain approved, Greece would acquire the Ionian Islands, a British possession for the past forty-eight years.

The points made by Prince Christian were shrewd and far-sighted. Deftly Sir Augustus Paget, the diplomat who had handled the Prince of Wales's marriage negotiations, sought to reassure him. Prince William, his father was told, could rely on the protection of the Powers, on British goodwill, on the cession of Corfu and the other Ionian Islands, and on a guaranteed income, in case he should be forced to return to Denmark. Otho, still refusing to abdicate, might style himself 'King of Greece' (Hellas) but the newcomer would be 'King of the Hellenes', a title which emphasized the popular and elective origin of the monarchy and asserted a claim to sovereignty over all the Greek peoples, whether living within the kingdom's frontiers or not. On 6 June 1863 King Frederick received a Greek delegation at the Charlottenborg Palace in the presence of Prince William, who had been rapidly promoted from cadet to naval captain for the occasion. The Prince formally accepted the delegation's offer of the crown of the Hellenes, choosing to be known by the last of his names, George, as a word more familiar in Greece than William. The National Assembly in Athens, unwilling to see the new reign begin under a regency, declared King George of age on 27 June, when he was still six months short of his eighteenth birthday. As there was already tension between rival factions in politics and the army, it was recognized that the King should travel to Athens as speedily as possible in the hope that his presence would strengthen the unity of his realm. During those troubled months of 1863 few would have thought it possible for Greece's young and inexperienced ruler to remain on his throne for almost half a century.

Shortly before midnight on Thursday, 29 October, the firing of rockets and blue flares off Piraeus let the people of Athens know that their King had reached the waters where, so many centuries ago, the war triremes manoeuvred on the eve of Salamis. His ship, the *Hellas*, anchored overnight, with a small flotilla of Greek and foreign vessels around her. At nine o'clock on Friday morning the *Hellas* steamed into port, closely followed by the French warship *Algeciras* and by HMS *Revenge*. It was just thirty-two weeks since Prince William had watched his sister step into the royal limelight of England; now the welcoming cheers and bunting were to honour him as *Vassilias Yeoryios*; and he stepped ashore almost as soon as the *Hellas* reached the quay. 'At the landing stage', a correspondent reported to the *Malta Times*, 'an Ionic temple of lath and calico had been erected – a capital and successful imitation of the real thing. Bowing gracefully round to the admiring crowd' the King 'entered his carriage, or rather the carriage of one of the Piraeus merchants, which had been purchased for the occasion, Otho's carriages having been sold'.

The local merchants fared well that day; for the King, with his escort of lancers, headed a procession of no less than ten such carriages along the road from Piraeus to Athens. It was a five-mile route and in those days followed the line of the northern 'long wall' of Periclean Athens. For the first time King George saw Greek vineyards and that early progeny of an ancient soil, the olive groves on the plain of the lower Kifissos. As his carriage approached the street named after Hermes, another improvised temple awaited him, this time decorated with Danish and Greek emblems. Similar devices were intertwined with green boughs along the balconies of low houses, backed by the monumental majesty of the Acropolis. The King stepped down outside the cathedral, where he was received by ten bishops; a *Te Deum* was sung; and he 'reverently kissed the Holy Gospels'. Then on to the largest building in the modern town, Otho's marble and limestone palace, fronted by an Ionic colonnade so shiningly new that it seemed to hold a promise of modern convenience, which was never quite fulfilled. There was as yet no floodlighting to illuminate past glories, but on that night Athenians and newcomers alike could see the eternal tranquillity of the Parthenon

13

Left Queen Louise of Denmark (1817–98), mother of George I, daughter of the Landgrave of Hesse-Cassel and of Princess Louise Charlotte of Denmark. It is through her that her husband, Christian IX, inherited the crown.

Below The arrival of George I at Piraeus, 30 October, 1863. 'At the landing stage an Ionic temple of lath and calico had been erected, a capital imitation of the real thing', ran a contemporary newspaper report.

presiding over the city. For, as the *Malta Times* reported, 'small dishes of resin and earth, were placed along the whole parapet which, when lighted, had the effect from the town of an encircling ring of fire'.

At noon next day – Saturday, 31 October – the King, in admiral's uniform, was received by the National Assembly. Speaking Greek publicly for the first time, he took his oath as sovereign of the Hellenes: 'In the name of the consubstantial and indivisible Trinity I swear to protect the dominant religion of the Greeks, to maintain and to defend the independence, the autonomy and the integrity of the Greek state, and to observe its laws.' A salute of 101 guns let the townsfolk of Athens and Piraeus, villagers clustered beneath Lycabettos, herdsmen and shepherds out on Hymettos and the marble quarrymen as far distant as Pentelikon all know that the reign of King George 1 had begun. To celebrate the occasion, there followed three days of official holiday.

King George was determined to avoid the pitfalls which had unseated Otho. He chose to be guarded by Greeks, not by detachments from the Protecting Powers; and, rather than appear aloof, he set about ensuring that his subjects recognized their monarch as an approachable man, an outsider who on their behalf was eager to become an insider. A correspondent of *The Times* noted within a month of the King's arrival in Athens that 'His Majesty makes numerous excursions on foot and horseback – sometimes in a small phaeton which he drives himself, generally only accompanied by 2 officers on duty.' Presumably he had an interpreter in discreet attendance, for the report continues: 'He walks through the streets alone on foot or with one of his young Danish friends, saluting all – stopping to converse with people, visiting the vegetable market inquiring the price of the articles for sale etc. King Otho, on the contrary, never went out at all but with the greatest solemnity.'

The same correspondent noted with warm approval that, again unlike his Roman Catholic predecessor, the King 'attends the national divine service on Sundays'. He showed such interest in the religious practices of his subjects that it was rumoured he was about to accept the Orthodox faith. This report *The Times* found hard to credit, and rightly. For, as the King's sons were to recall in their memoirs, George 1 remained a Lutheran believer, reading regularly from the bible he had brought with him from Denmark. But he respected his subjects' veneration of holy icons, acknowledged the wisdom of a constitutional provision that his heirs and successors must belong to the Greek Church, and insisted that members of his family should share in the sacramental mysteries of Orthodoxy. Only during Holy Week was it noticed that the King liked to slip away from Athens to Corfu or one of the quieter royal homes, where the rigours of religious observance were less intrusive or exacting.

Seventeen days after King George landed in Greece, his father acceded to the Danish throne as King Christian ix. There followed two terrible years for Denmark, culminating in war with Prussia and Austria and the loss of Schleswig-Holstein. The crisis in northern Europe intensified King George's personal isolation, for his Danish friends hurried home to serve their fatherland, leaving him to develop skills of his own as an impartial referee of faction fights between the rival politicians. No other king in Europe, summoned unexpectedly to a foreign throne, has ever had such responsibilities thrust on him at so early an age. In later years King George admitted to one of his sons that he had felt he was living on the slopes of a volcano. But he showed courage and resolution. Even before he arrived in Greece the National Assembly had begun to prepare a new constitution; the debate continued throughout his earliest months in the kingdom, preventing the passage of urgent measures to improve the economy. At last the young King lost his patience. Asserting his royal prerogative for the first time, he insisted that the draft constitution be put to the vote. Otherwise he would return to Denmark.

Thus, exactly a year after he took his oath in the Assembly, the form of the constitution was finally agreed. It received royal approval on 18 November 1864; and the Hellenic peoples – even those beyond the existing frontiers – were formally united politically in a 'democracy under a king' (*vasilevoméni dimokratia*). The assurance of direct, secret and universal male suffrage for a single chamber of parliament made Greece, at least on paper, one of the most democratic states in Europe. The King needed the advice and written support of his ministers for acts bearing his name; he had the right to form governments without dependence on any voting strength in parliament, although by 1875 he had come to recognize the wisdom of choosing as prime minister a party leader reasonably confident of support in the chamber. Ballot problems in an electorate with a high level of illiteracy and liable to intimidation by local brigands, difficulties in securing fair elections for residents abroad, and the absence of a clear-cut party system were to make the working of the 1864 constitution cumbersome, and in 1911 it was drastically amended. But the young king tried to make the 1864 model work. Between 1864 and 1911 he appointed 70 governments, their leadership shared between 17 rival prime ministers who 'went to the people' in 21 general elections (on the average, once every 6 months for the first 18 years of the reign, and thereafter once every 2 years 5 months). Small wonder that when George's third son wrote his memoirs in the 1920s he remembered that his father had grown accustomed to working a ten-hour day.

In the spring of 1864 he boarded the frigate *Hellas* again at Kalamata and, escorted by British, French and Russian warships, sailed northwards into the bay off Katakolon, the coastal plain backed by the wooded groves above Olympia. Southwards into the bay sailed the wooden three-decker HMS *Duke of Marlborough*. An admiral's barge pulled across to the *Hellas*; the British High Commissioner for the Ionian Islands was piped aboard; and, to the thunder of cannon from the massive ship of the line, Queen Victoria's representative handed over to the King of the Hellenes the flag which had flown over the Commissioner's residence in Corfu. By this exchange of ceremonial courtesies Corfu, Kephalonia, Zanthe, Ithaca and all other territories within 'the United States of the Ionian Islands' became an integral part of the Greek kingdom.

Apart from such voyages along coastal waters, for over three years George I never left his kingdom. He perfected his mastery of Greek; he travelled to the islands as well as into the Peloponnese and up to the border with the Ottoman Empire – which in 1863 still followed the frontier agreed thirty years before and ran from the Gulf of

Left *Grand Duke Constantine of Russia (1827–92), second son of Tsar Nicholas I and father of Queen Olga. He served for many years as General-Admiral of the Russian Navy and was a man of culture, interested in literature, science and music. Politically he was a progressive reformer encouraging his brother, Alexander II, to practise similar ideas.*

Right *The famous beauty Grand Duchess Alexandra (1830–1911), mother of Queen Olga, was born a Princess of Saxe-Altenburg. With her is her second son, Constantine (1858–1915), who became a much-praised writer.*

Left *George I with his 16-year-old fiancée, Grand Duchess Olga, at St Petersburg in 1867. Her sister Grand Duchess Vera (1854–1912), aged 13, is seated on the floor.*

Right *The young Queen Olga in traditional Russian costume.*

Arta eastwards to the Gulf of Volos, barely 130 miles north of Athens. The strangest contrast with his native Denmark, apart from the climate, was in the character of urban life. There had been only 300 houses in Athens when it became the seat of government in 1834. Pioneer street planning by a German architect held promise for the future, just as Queen Amalia's royal gardens had shown how careful horticulture could bring the beauty of a park to the stark wasteland on the edge of the town. Yet, despite the street markets which King George had already found buzzing with noisy vitality, nowhere in Greece was there any sense of metropolitan community. In Copenhagen Prince William was accustomed to life in a city of 158,000 people; King George's Athens had a population of 45,000. It was a conglomerate of villages spawned at the feet of newly cherished antique monuments. Not least among the King's achievements was to have encouraged in his capital the growth of a corporate urban life.

When eventually King George felt able to travel abroad he set out for Russia in search of a bride. His sister Dagmar married the Tsarevich Alexander, the eldest surviving son of Alexander II, in St Petersburg in November 1866. The Tsar's only daughter was too young for marriage, and eventually became the wife of Prince Alfred, Duke of Edinburgh. But King George's new brother-in-law had an attractive first cousin, Grand Duchess Olga, whom the King first met by chance while paying a courtesy call on her parents at Pavlovsk. She could not speak Danish or Greek and he knew no Russian, but both their mothers were German princesses by birth and in that language they pursued a discreet courtship. They were married in a splendid ceremony at St Petersburg on 27 October 1867, seven weeks after the Grand Duchess's sixteenth birthday. When King George brought his bride back to Athens 'a whole family of dolls' travelled with her. 'She wore', her youngest son writes, 'a little dress in the Greek colours of blue and white, and the crowds in the streets shouted themselves hoarse in welcome. Her shy youth and beauty conquered their impressionable hearts that day and, through all the vicissitudes of our house, she at least never lost their love.'

Queen Olga was still only sixteen when, on 2 August 1868, her first son was born. There was little doubt over the name he should bear. His mother's father was the Grand Duke Constantine, a name first introduced into the Romanov family in 1779 on Catherine the Great's insistence at a time when her armies were winning such triumphs against the Turks that she began to dream of a new Byzantine dynasty to reign beside the Bosphorus. For the Greeks, too, the name had a deep significance, recalling both 'the new Rome' in the East and the Emperor Constantine XI Paleologus who had died fighting in defence of Byzantine Orthodoxy on the day that the Turks breached the walls of Constantinople. Moreover, since the 1850s, Greek patriots had found inspiration in the *Megáli Idéa* (the 'Great Idea'), a creed which preached the need for action to unite the Hellenic peoples and which looked ultimately to the proclamation of a Greek empire at Constantinople itself. No other baptismal name could have been so heavy with portent. The subsequent creation of a dukedom of Sparta for the Crown Prince associated the new dynasty with yet another great epoch from the Greek past.

Great Britain's surrender of the Ionian Protectorate to Greece gave the royal family two homes on Corfu: an imposing three-storeyed palace of Malta stone built as the formal residence of the Lord High Commissioner; and the far more attractive summer residence of *Mon Repos*, a villa completed in 1824, set among olive, lemon and orange trees, cypresses and magnolias and looking out over the town, towards the Venetian citadel. King George and Queen Olga would retire to Corfu in the spring and summer months, and their second and third children were both born on the island: Prince George in June 1869; Princess Alexandra in August of the following year. But the royal family needed a retreat closer to Athens, and in 1871 the King purchased from his private funds a wooded estate at Tatoi, fifteen miles north of the capital. Hills on the edge of the estate once commanded an old route to Euboea and looked out across the plain to the blue edge of the Saronic Gulf; the Spartans had constructed a fortress above Tatoi at the end of the fifth century. King George built a small villa in which it was possible for his family to relax happily. Between 1886 and 1888 a far larger house went up close to the villa; it became, as Prince Nicholas was to write, 'our real home, where everybody was free to do as he liked'. There, his youngest brother Prince Christopher adds, 'We could forget that we were not supposed to be ordinary human beings.'

In earlier years the King and his young wife were 'ordinarily human' in Athens and Corfu, too. George I enjoyed roller-skating and bicycling, both inside and outside the palace. When Princess Alexandra made her first visit to Athens in June 1869, brother and sister slipped easily back to the teasing playfulness of childhood: a British equerry was surprised to see King George, with the neatest of footwork, dribbling the Princess of Wales's hat along a path in the royal gardens, followed by a laughing princess in mock angry pursuit; and a few days later on Corfu the King and the Prince of Wales, always the best of friends, fought a duel with over-ripe oranges in the gardens of *Mon Repos*. When, a few years later, King George came to London, the Prince gave a splendid dinner in his honour at Marlborough House. It was on this occasion that Sir Charles Dilke heard a well-wined Greek colonel, serving as an equerry for the visit, give considered opinions on his monarch and their host: 'He's a good little King, but not what I call a fashionable King', and pointing at the Prince of Wales, 'Now that's what I call a fashionable Prince.... He goes to bed late, it is true, but he gets up – well, never! ... My King gets up at six!'

The ties binding royal Europe together grew tighter as the families of King George and his two sisters passed from infancy into childhood. Queen Olga gave birth to her third son, Prince Nicholas, in January 1872 and her second daughter, Princess Marie, in March 1876, both in Athens. A third daughter, baptized Olga, was born four years later but lived for only six months. By then King George's sister, Dagmar, now Empress Marie of Russia, was the mother of three grand dukes and a grand duchess: her eldest son – later Tsar Nicholas II – became a close friend of his cousin, George of Greece, a year his junior. In May 1891 the tall and powerfully built Prince George was to save Nicholas's life in Japan by deflecting an assassin's sabre blow with his

19

Left An evzone attendant pushes the future King Constantine I around the palace gardens in a baby carriage once used for his mother, Queen Olga.

Right Queen Olga at the age of 53. Very short sighted since her youth she was never without her lornettes, which she used to her advantage as an elegant accessory.

stout walking stick.

In England the King's favourite sister, Princess Alexandra, had two sons and three daughters. Both of Princess Alexandra's sons – 'Eddy' (Prince Albert Victor) and 'Georgie' (Prince George of Wales) – visited Greece in May 1882 as midshipmen completing a voyage around the world in HMS *Bacchante*. They spent ten days at Tatoi with 'Uncle Willy, darling Aunt Olga & cousins', as the sixteen-year-old Prince George wrote in his diary. Georgie became a great favourite with his aunt and uncle. When their shore leave ended and it was time to return to *Bacchante*, 'We all cryed very much.' But the close friendship lingered on. The Prince received letters from his uncle containing porcine Danish endearments, such as *gamle polse* (my old sausage) or *gamle sylte* (my old pickled pork); and in his Aunt Olga's affectionate vocabulary the future King George V progressed slightly unexpectedly from 'my little sunbeam' to 'tootsums'. In that spring of 1882 there was a new baby in the Tatoi nursery, Prince Andrew, born just thirteen weeks before *Bacchante* sailed into Piraeus. Sixty-five years later the baby's son, Philip, and the midshipman's granddaughter, Elizabeth, were to marry in Westminster Abbey.

The Greek royal family became accustomed to long visits by sea or by train to western Europe and to Russia. They would stay at Fredensborg in Denmark,

King Christian IX of Denmark plays whist with his daughters: Alexandra, Princess of Wales; Empress Marie Feodorovna of Russia; Thyra, Duchess of Cumberland.

Gmunden in Austria, or one of the imperial palaces near Tsarskoe Selo; in August 1888 Queen Olga gave birth to her youngest son, Prince Christopher, at Pavlovsk. Their Danish and Russian kinsfolk would come frequently to Athens, too; Prince Nicholas retained a vivid memory of going aboard the Russian battleship *Svetlana* when he was four years old, not least because she was commanded by Grand Duke Alexis, an intimidating giant of a man. From 1884 onwards – when Prince Constantine was officially proclaimed *Diadoch* (Successor) and went to Germany to complete his education – there were increasing contacts with the Prussian Royal House, too.

These dynastic links supplemented the diplomacy of Europe's chancelleries. But Greece was slow to benefit from them. Successive British governments remained sympathetic to the Ottoman Empire while in St Petersburg there was constant suspicion of Greek dreams of a crusade 'to the city', the ambition to end the dominance of Islam in Constantinople. After 1870 the Russians preferred Panslavism to Orthodoxy as an ideological weapon against the Turks. The climax of the Russo-Turkish war of 1877–8 was a moment of great disillusionment for King George. During the Russian advance southwards through Bulgaria the King maintained a regular correspondence with the Tsar's commander-in-chief, Grand Duke Nicholas. The Russians were left in no doubt of Greek enthusiasm for a war to free Thessaly, Epirus and even Macedonia. As the King was celebrating his thirty-second birthday, he received constant news of armed bands crossing the Turkish frontier. A week later, in the first days of January 1878, he authorized partial mobilization. Finally on 1 February he ordered the army to march into Thessaly. But, to the King's dismay, despite his close marriage links with the Romanovs, he found Tsar Alexander II personally hostile to the Greek initiative. Peace, the Tsar insisted, must be dictated in San Stefano by Russia alone. Moreover, although Britain and France opposed Russian designs on Turkey, they, too, had no wish to see the European balance disturbed by Greek intervention. The King was forced to halt the advance of his troops. By 7 February they were back where they had started. The Treaty of Berlin promised Greece a rectification of her northern frontier. But only after George I ordered a second mobilization and again threatened war with Turkey in 1881 were Thessaly and a small segment of Epirus added to his kingdom.

King George was naturally cautious, preventing the machinery of mobilization from running away with him each time hotheaded nationalists called for war. He was prepared quietly to use his own diplomatic skills. Significantly, when the next eastern crisis began in September 1885, with the creation of an independent and unified Bulgaria, he was already in Vienna and able to sound out the opinion of the Emperor Francis Joseph and his ministers. He could see that the Great Powers would not tolerate a war to liberate Ioannina, however high feelings might run in Athens. And to emphasize the objections of the Protecting Powers, on 8 May the British imposed a three-week blockade on Greece. Ironically the commander of the naval squadron was Prince Alfred, Duke of Edinburgh, whom 230,000 Greeks had once voted their first choice as king.

Even if, on this occasion, the British presence may have helped the King check the

An informal group in a Danish palace, c. 1895. Queen Louise reads a letter while her daughters, the Princess of Wales and the Dowager Empress of Russia, stand between two of their Greek nephews, Prince George and his youngest brother, Prince Christopher.

Breakfast group in Denmark: Christian IX with two of his daughters, Queen Alexandra and Princess Thyra, faces his son, George I, across the table.

rash exuberance of his prime minister, it is hard to escape the impression that the behaviour of the Protecting Powers in each successive crisis was arrogant and patronizing. A hot-tempered and less patient ruler might have harboured a proud resentment at such interference. King George, however, remained stubbornly equable. Exactly twelve months after Prince Alfred's squadron left Greek waters, he was in London for the celebrations of Queen Victoria's Golden Jubilee. At the 'large family dinner' in Buckingham Palace on 20 June, the King sat on Queen Victoria's right and his father, as King of Denmark, on her left. Thereafter Victoria's sympathy for the sorely tried Greek monarchy never wavered.

Present also at the Golden Jubilee celebrations were 'Fritz' and 'Vicky', the German Crown Prince, Frederick William, (already suffering from cancer of the throat) and the Crown Princess Victoria, the Queen's eldest daughter. A close friendship, rooted in sympathetic understanding, developed between the Crown Princess – so soon, and so briefly, to be an empress – and the Greek sovereigns. The Empress Frederick was at times puzzled by the family's boisterous behaviour, particularly in the summer of 1889 when she encountered them on holiday in Copenhagen. King George's two eldest sons were 'the finest of the young men, and also the most intelligent', she wrote to her mother, adding that they were 'as strong as two young Hercules': 'The noise they all made and the wild romps they had were simply indescribable. Once or twice I was obliged to laugh right out when they were all carrying each other. They seemed happier and to enjoy themselves more than children of five or six.'

A month later the elder Hercules became her son-in-law. Prince Constantine, Duke of Sparta, had been in Germany for most of the years 1884–7, first at Heidelberg and

Queen Alexandra, George 1's favourite sister, with whom he corresponded at least once a week until his death.

Royal card players in Denmark, c. 1889. The future Constantine 1 and his brother, Prince George (then a naval cadet in Denmark) sit on either side of the still unbearded, future Tsar Nicholas 11, whose young brother George (1871–99) is sitting on the wall. Their British cousins, the Duke of Clarence and one of his sisters, seem more familiar with the game.

later serving with a Prussian Guards regiment in Potsdam and Hanover. At Potsdam he had met and admired Princess Sophie of Prussia, who was slightly less than two years his junior. Elaborate preparations were made for the young couple's wedding in Athens, the greatest social event in the city for many centuries. It was arranged to coincide with the twenty-second anniversary of the marriage of King George and Queen Olga, on 27 October. As well as the widowed Empress Frederick and her two unmarried daughters, the bride's brother the new Emperor Wilhelm 11 (the Kaiser) and Empress Augusta Viktoria came from Germany; the bridegroom's grandparents, the King and Queen of Denmark, had made the long journey from Copenhagen; and the Tsarevich Nicholas headed a large family contingent from St Petersburg. The Prince and Princess of Wales were accompanied by their eldest son, by now Duke of Clarence; but, despite the presence of the British Mediterranean Squadron in Phaleron Bay, Prince Alfred was not there. He was obliged, over the same weekend, to attend the funeral obsequies of King Luis the Good in Portugal. They continued for ten hours.

In Athens the marriage service lasted a mere hour: 'solemn and impressive', the bride's mother thought, but 'very long'. 'All the arrangements were very well made. The King himself had settled everything,' she reported to Queen Victoria, 'All has gone off very well.' Blue skies, with the weather warm enough for open carriages and 'low gowns' but, as it was the last Sunday in October, there was a pleasant light breeze blowing. The Empress Frederick was evidently intrigued by the gathering of bishops with their 'round mitres and long beards' and by the liturgical need for bride and bridegroom 'to walk three times round the altar' with 'a lighted candle each'. There followed a Protestant service in the 'nice little chapel here', a blessing, a prayer and two short chorales. The royal wedding captured the attention of the foreign press, as so often on later occasions. 'The long prepared-for wedding of the Duke of Sparta and the Princess Stephanie (*sic*) of Prussia took place on Sunday last in the Cathedral at Athens', the *Church Times* reported, almost correctly, in London. 'The gorgeous ceremonial of the Greek Church must have astonished some of the many German Lutherans, even as the bald Protestant ceremony which succeeded must have perplexed the native members of the Orthodox Greek Church.'

But these perplexities, if they existed, were soon forgotten in the festive mood of royal court and people. The celebrations began under the thunder of saluting cannon and continued against a background concatenation of pealing bells from all the churches. It was twenty-six years, almost to the day, since the young bachelor king first stepped ashore at Piraeus. Among living sovereigns only Franz Josef of Austria-Hungary and Queen Victoria had reigned longer than George I. With five sons, two daughters and now a daughter-in-law the dynasty seemed as secure as any in Europe – provided always that the sovereign lived up to the proud affirmation on the royal coat of arms, 'My Strength is the Love of My People'.

George I wearing the insignia of the Order of the Garter, with which he was invested by Queen Victoria in 1876.

2

THE EXPANSION
OF THE KINGDOM

Unless he saw inept policies threatening the kingdom with disaster, George i never intervened in the day-to-day conduct of government. But, like all far-sighted monarchs, he gave powerful backing to major projects of development. Greece was a late starter in the railway age; he had been on the throne for six years before the first line was opened, and then it ran only from Athens to Piraeus. The acquisition of Thessaly in 1881 stimulated hopes of a through link with western Europe and in 1884 the King's inauguration of the Volo-to-Larissa line caused more excitement than the 38-mile track technically warranted. But the King's main interest had always been in the encouragement of a mercantile fleet and, in particular, the building of a canal across the isthmus of Corinth, a project which had interested the emperors Caligula and Nero eighteen centuries before. King George made the first symbolic incision of a spade in the hard limestone in the spring of 1882, but it was not until August 1893 that he opened the canal, with the bow of the royal yacht breaking ribbons in the national colours of blue and white which were festooned between the moles on either side of the entrance. The opening of the canal cut a sea voyage to Piraeus from the Adriatic ports by over 150 miles and from Malta or the Straits of Messina by about eighty miles. It revived trading communities along the Gulf of Corinth and saved ships from the often stormy waters off Cape Matapan.

The King also gave his patronage to the movement for reviving the Olympic Games, although in Athens rather than at their original home in Elis. He had already encouraged the initiative of Ernst Ziller in clearing the site of the fourth-century stadium where the Panathenaic Games were once contested; and in 1894–5 he backed both Baron de Coubertin's campaign to arouse interest in the Games and the efforts of Anastasios Metaxas to restore the Pentelic marble stadium, with generous benefactions from the financier, George Averoff. The first Olympiad of the modern era was a pleasantly informal gathering of genuine amateurs from twelve nations. It received warm support from the King, who was seated beside King Alexander (Obrenović) of Serbia on that memorable day in October 1896 when some 75,000 onlookers willed the barefooted Spyros Louy, a shepherd from the hilltop village of Amarousion seven miles outside Athens, into the stadium to win the gruelling run from Marathon. 'What nationality is the victor?' asked the short-sighted King Alexander. 'From the cheers of the crowd I think he must either be a Turk or a Bulgarian,' his neighbour drily replied. The King's second son, George – at six foot six inches 'the tallest Prince in Christendom' – hurried down from the stadium to run beside Louy for the last thousand yards. Thereafter the royal family has kept faith with Coubertin's ideal of helping 'the Olympic flame' to 'shine through all generations'. In 1906 the King supported the holding of a tenth-anniversary Games in the now fully completed stadium and fifty-four years later his great-grandson won a gold medal in the yachting contests at Naples. The King's descendants in the British royal family were to make contributions to the equestrian events of later Olympics.

In 1896 Louy's triumph in this first Marathon came as a welcome fillip to Greek national pride. Patriotic feelings were already running high that year, for in the previous spring an insurrection had broken out in Crete against Turkish misrule in the island. At the time of the Olympics an uneasy truce enveloped Crete: the Sultan had appointed a Christian governor and, in August, authorized further concessions to his non-Muslim subjects. But early in February 1897 there was further violent unrest: the Greek consul in Khania warned Athens by telegraph that the Christians were about to be massacred; a committee of Cretan revolutionaries declared the island absorbed into the Kingdom of the Hellenes; and King George ordered his second son, who had received his naval training in Denmark, to sail from Salamis with four torpedo boats and take possession of the island.

Prince George's flotilla reached the approaches to Khania before daybreak on Friday, 12 February. The ships sailed again for home waters on Saturday afternoon. The King had long hoped that his valuable dynastic connections would negotiate the transfer of Crete peacefully; and it is probable that, before Prince George withdrew, he knew he could count on the backing of the Tsar for proposals to have the Prince appointed governor-general of the island. In Athens, however, Prime Minister Theodore Deligiannis, his political colleagues and the more junior army officers were impatient. Foolishly they allowed their patriotic ardour to outpace diplomacy. Fifteen hundred armed volunteers sailed from Piraeus to support the insurrection as if emulating the achievements of Garibaldi's Thousand in Sicily during the Italian Risorgimento.

But, though George I possessed greater political insight than Piedmont's Victor Emmanuel II, Deligiannis was no Cavour. The Prime Minister not only encouraged the filibustering expedition to Crete, but also turned a blind eye to raids by irregular bands across the Turkish borders into Thessaly. Anxious messages from the Empress Frederick, from Queen Victoria and from the Tsar urged King George to hold Greece back from war with Turkey, for the Sultan had sufficient reserves to put a million men into the field, well-equipped and trained by German specialist officers. King George could not stand out against the crusading spirit of the Athenians: in case of war, the Greeks would rise against Turkish oppression throughout the Sultan's lands and other nationalities would follow their example, the King told the Gladstonian

Liberal churchman, Canon MacColl, in Athens that spring. So serious were the incursions into Thessaly that Turkey declared war on Greece in the third week of April. No wave of insurrection shook the Ottoman Empire.

The Thirty Days War was humiliating for Greece and almost disastrous for the dynasty. 'The Turks are a fearful foe,' the dowager Empress Frederick wrote to her mother at the start of the war, 'Like beasts in their cruelty'; she was indignant with her son, the Kaiser, for supporting the Turks and deeply worried over the fate of her daughter, Crown Princess Sophie, whose husband was receiving his baptism of fire as commander-in-chief; 'There will be no more sleep for me now for days', the Empress added. Turkish troops based on Ellasona, south-west of Mount Olympus, thrust the Greeks back from the Meluna Pass and advanced on the Diadoch's headquarters in Larissa. Prince Nicholas was commanding an artillery battery when the war began. He was astonished at the rapid spread of demoralization among the hard-pressed troops. Good Friday – 23 April, the King's name day – stood out in his memory: 'In a few minutes the Army, from an organized and disciplined unity, was transformed into a seething disorganized mass of fugitives that sped helter-skelter across the plain, back to Larissa, a distance of almost forty miles.' That night it was recognized in the European capitals that Greece was facing defeat. Queen Victoria sent a telegram to Tsar Nicholas II urging him to mediate between the belligerents and supporting the proposal of her Prime Minister, Salisbury, that the 'three guarantors of Greece after Navarino' should take joint action to check the Turks. Eventually, on 10 May, King George reluctantly accepted an armistice, which required the withdrawal of Greek troops from Crete as well as a cease-fire in Epirus and on the plains of Pharsalla.

Queen Victoria also insisted that the Royal Navy should render aid, if necessary, to the Greek royal family, and the battleship HMS *Nile* was ordered to Phaleron Bay. The Protecting Powers finally secured a peace treaty at Constantinople in early December, allowing the Greeks to retain Thessaly, except for minor adjustments of the frontier in Turkey's favour around some twenty villages from the coastal plain beneath Mount Ossa westwards to Malakassa in the foothills of the Pindus; and Greece had to pay an indemnity to Turkey which the Kingdom could ill-afford. Unjustly, popular indignation was turned against the dynasty. On 26 February 1898 a muddle-headed anarchist named Kardzitis fired six rifle shots at King George as he drove in a carriage with Princess Marie along the road to Phaleron. Neither father nor daughter was hurt and the crime rallied support for the Crown. A church was built where the murder attempt had been made; crowds flocked there to give thanks for the King's deliverance. Kardzitis, who took to the mountains, was hunted down, put on trial and executed at Nauplion.

Meanwhile the Great Powers reached a compromise settlement over Crete. The last Turkish garrison withdrew in November 1898; an international contingent – British, French, Russian and Italian troops and marines – policed the island; and Prince George became High Commissioner in Khania. Although Crete remained an autonomous island in the Ottoman Empire, effectively it was linked with royal Greece

31

Left *George I's eldest daughter, Princess Alexandra, who married Grand Duke Paul, the youngest son of Tsar Alexander II, in 1889. She died in Moscow two years later, soon after her 21st birthday, after giving birth to a son, Dimitri, one of the future assassins of Rasputin.*

Below left *The 26-year-old Princess Marie of Greece in Russian costume for a ball at The Hermitage, St Petersburg, in 1903.*

Below *Princess Nicholas of Greece (Grand Duchess Elena of Russia), the mother of the three beautiful Princesses, Olga, Elisabeth and Marina.*

through the person of its highest dignitary. During his eight years of office Prince George's affability, enthusiasm and fair-mindedness made him popular with the peasantry. Only a small group of young politicians – headed by the 34-year-old lawyer, Eleftherios Venizelos – was uneasy at the Prince's coming. For them his administration remained too cautiously conservative over formal union with Greece.

Prince George was still a bachelor throughout his eight years in Crete. Other members of his family strengthened the dynastic links with Russia. His sister Alexandra had married her mother's first cousin, Grand Duke Paul, the youngest son of Tsar Alexander II, in 1889; she was, the Empress Frederick thought, a beautiful woman although pale and anaemic in appearance. She had a daughter, Grand Duchess Maria, born in April 1890, but she died seventeen months later, a few days after giving birth to a son. Despite this tragedy, in May 1900 her sister Princess Marie, a strong-willed Greek patriot, married another first cousin of their mother, Grand Duke George, at Corfu – having refused to go to Russia for her wedding, like other members of the family. Her two daughters, the Princesses Nina (born 1901) and Xenia (born 1903), spent most of their childhood in Greece and Great Britain as their mother did not enjoy life at the Tsar's court. On the other hand her brother, Prince Nicholas, who married Tsar Alexander II's granddaughter, Grand Duchess Elena, at Tsarskoe Selo in August 1902, regularly spent part of each summer in Russia: his two elder daughters, the Princesses Olga and Elisabeth, were however born at Tatoi in, respectively, June 1903 and May 1904; and in December 1906 his youngest daughter, Princess Marina – who was to bring such grace and style to London society thirty years later – was born in Athens.

King George I's fourth son, Prince Andrew, looked elsewhere than Russia for a bride. While in London in April 1903 he became engaged to Princess Alice of Battenberg. Six months later every member of the Greek royal family, nine Romanovs (including Nicholas II and the Tsarina), Queen Alexandra of England, a galaxy of Battenbergs and a princely ensemble from within Germany all converged on Darmstadt for the wedding, 260 guests in all. The Hessian ring of palaces in the wooded hills of the Odenwald had long been the most relaxed royal playground in Europe, and Princess Alice's marriage celebrations kept faith with this carefree Darmstadt tradition. 'More like a Bank Holiday on Hampstead Heath than royal ceremonial', a naval friend of the bride's father observed with astonishment. Princess Marie of Battenberg, on the other hand, thought 'the procession of their Greek Majesties with a military escort ... outriders and many pair-horsed carriages was splendid' and was glad that 'all the available magnificence of the Grand Ducal stables ... was brought into play'; but she, too, rejoiced at the 'happy, merry mood' in which 'various Majesties and Royal Highnesses ... threw rice and slippers' as the carriage of the bride and bridegroom pulled away.

Four months before this 'beautiful, happy day' in Hesse-Darmstadt, young army officers had burst into the old palace at Belgrade, fired some fifty bullets into the bodies of King Alexander (Obrenović) of Serbia and his Queen, hacked them with sabres and thrown their blood-stained and naked corpses from the window. King

The marriage of George I's younger daughter, Marie, to Grand Duke George Mikhailovich at Corfu, 12 May 1900. The pages in sailor suits appear to be two future Kings of Greece, George II (right) and Alexander (left).

George I had never liked his neighbour and knew the strength of support among the younger Serbs for the rival dynasty of Karadjordjević, but these revolting murders startled royal and imperial Europe. Emperors and kings were accustomed to the terrors of anarchism and red revolution; here, however, was a new phenomenon, the threat of an ambitious officer corps, linked for political objectives in a conspiratorial fraternity which treated with cynical contempt the oath of loyalty to the crown. Military pressure was not always exercised so drastically as in the Belgrade crime but, from 1903 onwards, it became a menace no government dared ignore, least of all in the Balkans. Some twenty years later one guest at the Darmstadt wedding, Prince Nicholas, could write with deep feeling that the infiltration of the army into the concerns of the state had become 'the curse of the Greek nation'.

Most threatened by a dissident officer corps was the Diadoch, Constantine, Duke of Sparta. The Crown Prince's married life remained happy. A son – the future King

Above A royal trio in Greek national costume on the balcony of the palace at Athens: Queen Olga, who restored the use of such dress at Court, is flanked by her daughter, Princess Marie and her daughter-in-law, Princess Andrew.

Left The youngest sons of George I: the Princes Andrew and Christopher.

George II – was born at Tatoi on 19 July 1890, shortly before the Diadoch's twenty-second birthday, and Queen Victoria was pleased to become one of the child's godmothers. There followed, in swift succession, Prince Alexander in August 1893 and Princess Helen in May 1896; later came Prince Paul in December 1901, Princess Irene in February 1904 and Princess Katherine in May 1913. But the Diadoch was a professional soldier, well trained in Prussia and full of admiration for the German General Staff created by the great Moltke. His personal relationship with the ruler of Germany, his brother-in-law Kaiser Wilhelm II, was, however, strained. At the time of her first child's birth, Crown Princess Sophie resolved to leave the Lutheran church and accept the Orthodox faith of her husband's future subjects; her imperial brother was, however, so hostile to the change of religion that he threatened never again to welcome her to Germany, a display of bigotry which prompted an epistolary rap on the knuckles from his grandmother at Windsor. Such a personal affront ran deeply in Athens and so, too, did the Kaiser's avowed partiality for the Sultan's army in the Thirty Days War. But the Diadoch was a realist. Even before the war, Empress Frederick had urged him 'to get help from our German army, it has such a good

35

The relics of Bishop Spiridion, patron saint of the island, are carried in procession before the royal family on the steps of the Palace of Saint George and Saint Michael at Corfu, April 1906. The silver reliquary was carried through the streets each year on Palm Sunday, Easter Eve, 11 August and the first Saturday in November.

organization'; and she had pointed out that General von der Goltz was achieving wonders with his training methods in Turkey. Bitter experience confirmed all his mother-in-law wrote. He despised Greek officers who had fallen short of the standards he saw in Germany, thereby making himself enemies. At the same time, he began to look for the nucleus of a personal staff, men of promise who would benefit from training in Prussia. By April 1906, when the future Queen Mary could record in her diary how she went sightseeing 'with the Tinos ... to the beautiful Acropolis', there were already factions in the officer corps, for or against the Diadoch.

In that year a new crisis in Crete threatened the stability of the kingdom. Prince George administered the island with tolerance and understanding, but he exasperated Venizelos by his failure to bring nearer the formal union of the island with the mainland kingdom. Faced with virtual civil war around Khania, Prince George resigned as High Commissioner and retired to Paris (where, a year later, he married Princess Marie Bonaparte, a great-great-niece of Napoleon I). Alexander Zaimis, a politician of tact and long experience, succeeded Prince George as High Commissioner and kept Crete smouldering rather than consumed by fire. But when in July 1908

Turkish army officers in the Committee of Union and Progress – the so-called 'Young Turks' – seized power in Constantinople pledged to the modernization of the Sultan's empire, it was impossible to restrain Greek patriots either in Athens or Crete. On 12 October 1908 the Cretan Assembly proclaimed the island united to Greece. But political leaders in Athens, and indeed the King himself, were too alarmed at the reaction of the Great Powers to welcome the Cretan action unreservedly. This inactivity aroused such anger in the Athens garrison that in May 1909 dissident junior officers established a Military League which three months later overthrew the Government.

The precise programme of Colonel Zorbas, head of the Military League, was never formulated. But the officers were uncompromisingly anti-dynastic, complaining in particular of speedy promotion accorded to the alleged 'favourites' of Crown Prince Constantine (who was at that time abroad). The royal princes resigned their commissions rather than see the Military League force their father to dismiss them from the army. But such an act could not prevent the officer corps from becoming deeply involved in factional politics. The careful improvement of staff work and training and the patient search in France, Germany and Britain for specialist equipment capable of carrying the army to victory in a Balkan campaign were abandoned. The Military League even demanded the dissolution of the General Staff. Had Greece been forced to wage war in 1910, the outcome would have been even more disastrous than thirteen years before.

During the autumn of 1909 *The Times* of London persistently carried reports that King George was about to abdicate. Such tales misjudged him. If foreign commentators underestimated the King's tenacity and courage, they also ignored his sense of mission. For George I shared the conviction held by so many rulers of his generation that kingship, whether mystic and sacramental or merely contractual in origin, raises the monarch above party bickering and entrusts to his protection the political assets in a state which doctrinaire reformers would squander. It is to George I's credit that, when Zorbas and his nominees failed to govern effectively, he was prepared to send for a politician, acceptable to the Military League, who had shown scant respect for the dynasty. With his long experience of handling prime ministers, the King realized that Venizelos, for all his shortcomings, combined in these years shrewd skills in statecraft with a glowing patriotic pride. 'My father, of all men, had the least cause to like him,' Prince Christopher was to write a quarter of a century later, 'yet the fact remains that he not only liked him, but trusted him.'

Venizelos agreed to form a government only on condition that the National Assembly revised the constitution, so as to prevent obstructive parliamentary tactics by minority groups, forbid serving officers from being deputies and permit social reform legislation to benefit the peasantry. With a parliamentary majority for his new Liberal Party and with the Military League in liquidation, Venizelos sought to restore confident leadership in the army. 'I consider that Lieutenant-General the Crown Prince is endowed with exceptional military abilities such as few senior officers possess,' Venizelos told parliament in June 1911; 'I look upon the Crown Prince as the most

37

suitable commander for the armed forces.' The Diadoch was at once reinstated and appointed Inspector-General of the army. The General Staff resumed its assessment of Balkan objectives, with Turkey as the most likely enemy and Macedonia and Epirus the most probable theatres of war; but even the merits of an assault on the Dardanelles were considered – briefly. A French military mission arrived in Athens; British naval advisers were welcomed at Salamis. Gunnery trials were held to test artillery from Schneider (France), Krupps (Germany) and Armstrong (Britain). The verdict went in favour of France. Next time there would be no precipitate rush into an ill-prepared campaign against an over-mighty neighbour.

George I's stature in Europe had grown rather than diminished during the crises which assailed him in the century's opening decade. In 1906 he had welcomed King Edward VII and Queen Alexandra on a state visit to Athens and he continued to travel regularly to Vienna, Gmunden and across Germany to Fredensborg and the tranquillity of Denmark where, on his father's death in January 1906, King George's brother acceded as Frederick VIII. Each year, too, the King would take the waters at Aix-les-Bains, a town he liked better than the fashionable spas of Bohemia. From 1907 onwards he met the German Emperor each spring on Corfu, where the Kaiser had purchased the Achilleion Villa, originally the home of the Empress Elizabeth of Austria. William II was entranced by the beauty of the island and elated by the discovery that his villa was close to the site of a temple of Artemis. George I, although still glad to escape to *Mon Repos* each April, would have preferred the peace unshattered by hearty visits from a holidaying Hohenzollern. 'Then why go to Corfu while he is there?' Queen Olga sensibly asked. 'If I don't, he'll think *he* is the King of Greece,' her husband replied.

He met the Kaiser, too, on that May morning in 1910 when he was one of nine kings who followed Edward VII's funeral cortège from Westminster Hall to Paddington Station. These sad days in London and Windsor also gave George I, the senior monarch present, an opportunity for conversation with his Balkan neighbours: Crown Prince Alexander of Serbia, who was involved in a running fight with Belgrade's equivalent of a Military League, he hardly knew; but he was well aware of the pretensions of 'Foxy Ferdinand', who, after twenty-one years as Prince of Bulgaria, in October 1908 had proclaimed himself 'Tsar of the Bulgarians', an imperial grandeur cut to king-size outside his realm. It was rumoured that in Sofia the full regalia of a Byzantine Emperor was kept locked in a chest, ready for the proud day when Ferdinand should enter Constantinople. More immediately, however, King Ferdinand wished to expand his territories so as to annexe much of Macedonia (where the Greeks and Serbs were also active) and southwards to the Aegean where Salonika,

Left above George I escorts his sister, Queen Alexandra, into the marble stadium at Athens in April 1906 for the Games celebrating the 10th anniversary of the first Olympiad; Edward VII follows, with Queen Olga. Behind them come the Princess of Wales, Crown Princess Sophie and Crown Prince Constantine, talking to the Prince of Wales (George V).

Far left George I walks with his sister, Queen Alexandra, around the gardens of the royal palace in Athens.

Left Edward VII in the long colonnade of the palace in Athens.

39

the second largest city in European Turkey, was a prize coveted as much by the Bulgarians as by the Greeks. Meetings between King George and King Ferdinand (a Coburger by birth) were always correct, but lacking in warmth.

Within eighteen months of Edward VII's funeral and only eleven weeks after the Diadoch resumed his work as Inspector-General, war came unexpectedly to the eastern Mediterranean. Italy, eager for colonial gains in North Africa, demanded the cession by the Sultan of his two Libyan provinces. Rejection of the ultimatum was followed by an Italo-Turkish War which dragged on for thirteen months: the Italian fleet was active in the Aegean and the southern Adriatic and, to the dismay of the government in Athens, the Italians occupied the Dodecanese, where the population was overwhelmingly Greek. The evident weakness of the Turks encouraged the Balkan nations to forget their differences in a united front which would seek to expel the Ottomans from Europe after five and a half centuries of Islamic rule. Unrest in Turkish Albania and reports of mutiny in Thrace and Macedonia led Montenegro, Serbia, Bulgaria and finally Greece to declare war on the Ottoman Empire in the second week of October 1912, just seven days before the firing ceased in the Italo-Turkish conflict.

King George was cautious; he accepted the need for a war of liberation only with reluctance, for he had bitter memories of the last occasion upon which Greek divisions crossed the Thessalian frontier. But this time the Balkan allies could put twice as many troops into the field as the Turks possessed in Europe; Crown Prince Constantine, acting in concert with Venizelos and the commander-in-chief of the fleet, Admiral Koundouriotis, was confident of success. The navy mopped up Turkish islands in the Aegean while the Diadoch's army advanced swiftly through the passes around Mount Olympus, reaching Katerini on 28 October, only ten days after the declaration of war. The decisive battle, named after the neighbouring town of Yiannitsa, was fought on 1 November outside the village of Melissi, where the Turks tried to prevent the Crown Prince's troops from crossing the River Balitsa. This victory, thirty-three miles west of Salonika, enabled the Greeks to cut the railway from the port to Monastir (now Bitolj) and the Serbian theatre of war. The Crown Prince's troops then marched on Salonika itself. Their entry into the city on 9 November was well-timed; it came on the eve of the festival of Salonika's patron saint, Demetrius; and it forestalled a determined effort by Greece's Balkan rival to filch the prize. For, only a few hours after Hassim Tahsim Pasha surrendered his sword to Constantine in the Konak – the Turkish administrative centre – a Bulgarian division reached Salonika's north-eastern outskirts. King George arrived by train two days later, but was at once up in the saddle to lead his victorious troops into the city, with the Diadoch and the royal

Left above Kaiser Wilhelm II lands at Corfu. George I told Queen Olga that he intended to be in Corfu whenever the Kaiser stayed at his villa because 'If I don't, he'll think he is King of Greece'.

Far left Aboard the Russian Imperial yacht: Crown Prince Constantine (second from right); Tsar Nicholas II (fifth from right).

Left Queen Olga and Crown Prince Constantine greet the French Empress Eugénie, who often visited Greece.

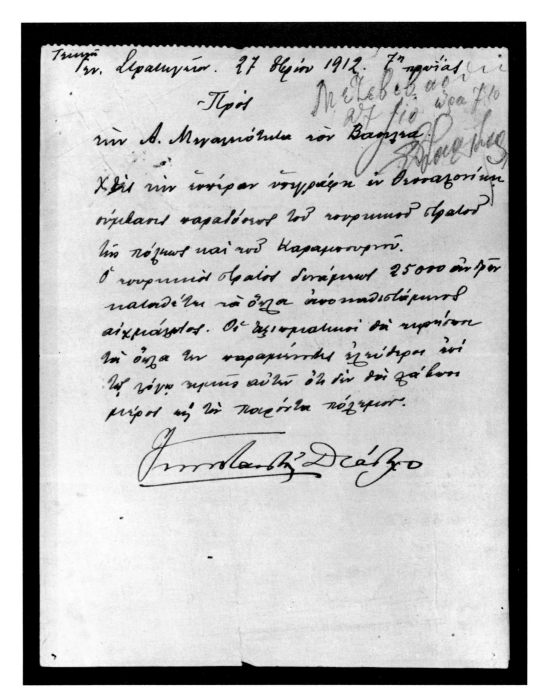

It was the Diadoch himself who wrote the message relating the important events of 27 October 1912 [9 November (NS)], later wired to the King:

'Yesterday evening, signed at Salonika, the agreement to surrender the Turkish army from the town and from Karabournou.

'The Turkish army, 25,000 men strong, was taken prisoner, delivered its arms. The officers kept their arms, remaining free under oath not to take part in the present war.'

Constantine I and senior officers during the Balkan Wars.

princes who had served on his staff following their father on horseback. Also present were two of the King's grandsons, the Princes George and Alexander, by now junior officers attached to their father's staff. For King George the entry into the city which he knew as Thessaloniki stood out as the proudest hour in a long reign.

The fighting continued in Epirus for another month while the Great Powers sought to negotiate an armistice. By the first week in December the war seemed over, with peace talks about to begin in London. The diplomats, however, made slow progress and the Turks denounced the armistice at the start of February 1913. Crown Prince Constantine set out from Salonika for field headquarters at Khani Emin Aga, high in the rugged mountains of Epirus, where the Greeks were besieging the rocky stronghold of Ioannina. Prince Nicholas remained in Salonika as Military Governor, with his father in residence at the Villa Allatini which a few months earlier had housed the deposed Sultan, Abdul Hamid. On 21 February, Prince Nicholas was able to give his father the news that Ioannina, too, had fallen to the Greeks. There would be much to celebrate in the King's Golden Jubilee festivities in June.

Prince Christopher, who was among his father's visitors during these triumphant days, says that the King planned to retire once the war was over, abdicating in favour of the architect of victory, his eldest son Constantine. But there was to be no Jubilee and no abdication. After lunching with Prince Nicholas on Tuesday, 18 March, King

43

Above *The funeral of George I in Athens, 3 August 1913. Among royal mourners led by Constantine I are Crown Prince Ferdinand of Romania, Prince Henry of Prussia, Crown Prince Alexander of Serbia, Crown Prince Boris of Bulgaria and Prince Alexander of Teck.*

Right *Constantine I honours the Colour standard of a Greek regiment after the early victories of the Balkan Wars.*

A hero's return from the Balkan Wars. Queen Sophie welcomes her husband, Constantine 1, as he disembarks at Phaleron.

George went for a late afternoon stroll, informally and almost unattended. About a mile to the east of the White Tower and some 200 yards from the foreshore, there was in 1913 an open space marked off by railings, over which it was possible to look out across the Thermaic Gulf to the majesty of Olympus picked out sharply by a setting sun. The King paused by these railings. As he turned away, a bystander pulled out a revolver and shot him in the back. A bullet penetrated the heart. He died instantly.

Prince Nicholas's immediate concern was to make it known that the assassin, Alexander Schinas, was a mentally disturbed Greek, not a Bulgarian or Turk. He

46

feared that innocent foreigners might be slaughtered in a wave of revenge. Schinas was never brought to trial, for he killed himself while in custody; he appears to have been an alcoholic who on that fateful day was gripped by a grievance which no one could understand. The new sovereign, King Constantine, came to Salonika by fast torpedo-boat across the Gulf, as the war itself seemed to pause in honour of the dynasty's founding father. Escorted, as on earlier ceremonial occasions, by British, French and Russian warships as well as by the victorious vessels of his own navy, George I's remains left Salonika by sea, and in a heavy fog. From Piraeus his coffin was taken to the cathedral in Athens. Finally his bones found rest, as he had wished, beneath the pines on Mount Paleocastro, above the royal estate at Tatoi.

A preliminary peace for the Balkans was signed in London on 30 May, confining Turkey-in-Europe to Constantinople and its hinterland and the Gallipoli peninsula. But the Bulgarians, who had suffered heavy casualties, felt cheated by the settlement. King Ferdinand, disappointed in his hopes of aggrandizement in Macedonia, ordered the Bulgarian army forward against the Greeks in the night of 29–30 June and there followed six days of fierce fighting. At first the Greeks lost the town of Gevgeli, but it was recaptured next day and the Bulgarians were soon forced to retreat around Lake Doiran and up the Rupel Pass. The Serbs, too, advanced into Bulgaria from the west and the Romanians from the north, while the Sultan's tattered army took the opportunity to recover the city of Edirne (Adrianople). A definitive settlement, the Treaty of Bucharest, was concluded between the Balkan states on 10 August; but it was not until 14 November that Turkey and Greece settled their new boundaries. The Greeks had to wait another three months before the Great Powers recognized their maritime mastery over the Aegean.

The final gains from these Balkan campaigns doubled the size of Greece. The whole of western Thrace, southern and western Macedonia, Crete and all the islands of the Aegean except the Dodecanese, Tenedos and Imbros were included within the Kingdom of the Hellenes. King Constantine, hailed on his return to Athens as a triumphant soldier hero, could begin his reign with a residue of popularity inconceivable during the bitter conflict with the Military League only five years before. 'The spring and summer of 1914 was the most carefree, the most prosperous that Greece had ever known,' Prince Christopher recalled nearly a quarter of a century later. 'I think we can at last look forward to peace,' King Constantine remarked to his youngest brother in June. It was the month in which, across the Balkan mountains, Archduke Francis Ferdinand of Austria had decided to visit Sarajevo on Serbia's national day.

Constantine I at German army manoeuvres looks out towards 'the enemy'. Behind him looms the younger General von Moltke (1848–1916), talking to Kaiser Wilhelm II. On the far right is General Papoulas, an outstanding Greek commander during the Balkan Wars.

3

A TRAGEDY OF
MISUNDERSTANDING

No monarch of recent times has suffered so malignantly from the barbed arrows of misfortune as the first King Constantine of the Hellenes. Soon after the outbreak of the First World War the French Foreign Office decided he was a 'Germanophile' and allied propaganda consistently attacked him as 'the Kaiser's friend and brother-in-law' throughout the following four years. Prince Nicholas, passing through London in the winter of 1916–17, was appalled at the hysteria with which the British press commented on his brother's policies; and when Lloyd George came to write his *War Memoirs*, more than ten years after Constantine's death, he dismissed him contemptuously as that 'surly and suspicious King of Greece, who was only too sympathetic to the Germans'. Sadly, these malevolent tales of treachery and deception created a legacy of misunderstanding accepted unquestioningly by public figures in London and Paris long after the fighting was over; they may even have influenced the opinion of political leaders during the Second World War and beyond. In Lloyd George's envenomed narrative it is impossible to recognize the king whom the most intransigently anti-German member of the British royal house, Queen Alexandra, could still call in 1920, 'poor, excellent, honest Tino'.

The origins of the Germanophile legend may be pinned down precisely in time, to the autumn of 1913. Less than three weeks after returning to Athens from the Macedonian front, King Constantine travelled to Germany, as a guest at army manoeuvres. While in Berlin he also hoped to negotiate a substantial loan to provide funds for developing the port of Salonika and constructing a railway northwards from Larissa into Greece's new territories. Over these projects the Germans were unhelpful; they were already pouring capital into the Ottoman Empire, and the German Foreign Ministry was at that moment uninterested in what happened in Athens. But Kaiser Wilhelm, conscious that Greece's historic Protectors were also the three Entente Powers, pursued a private policy of his own; he sought to entice the Greeks into close partnership. On the eve of the manoeuvres he gave a dinner in honour of King Constantine; the Kaiser praised his guest's military achievements which had made him worthy of the rank of field marshal. The King was flattered; his mother-in-law

Left *Three children of Constantine I on the roof of the royal palace in Athens, with Lycabettos in the background. They were to become King George II, Queen Helen of Romania and King Alexander.*

Below *An informal visit to Sandringham, in Norfolk as guests of Queen Alexandra: Constantine I (fourth from right) with his brother George, Princess Marie-Bonaparte, the Duchess of Aosta, Queen Marie of Romania, the Landgravine of Hesse and other members of the royal families of Europe.*

had always maintained that the German army and the British navy were the finest in the world; and, after the humiliations of the 1897 campaign and the derisive attacks of the Military League, he was proud to receive a field marshal's baton in so exclusive a community. In an impromptu speech of thanks the King showed his genuine pleasure at the compliments paid to him. He associated the German officer corps with the victories of Greece's armies in the recent war: he reminded his dining companions that he had himself been trained in Germany; his eldest son, returning to the homeland after two years service in a crack Prussian Guards regiment, had put the knowledge acquired at Potsdam into practice on the battlefields of Macedonia and Epirus; and, in recent years, many Greek staff officers had profited from their studies at the *Kriegsakademie*.

All this was true; and, so long as the King's comments remained the confidential knowledge of a select fraternity of officers, the speech was harmless. King Constantine attended the manoeuvres and then went on to England, for his youngest children attended private schools at Eastbourne. Prince Paul, who would be twelve in December 1913, was interested in a naval career rather than in following his brothers to military academies; and the King wished to discover if the Prince might become a naval cadet at Osborne or Dartmouth. While the King was in England press reports of his speech in Germany were summarized in *The Times*, prompting explanatory comments which the newspaper featured fully and fairly. Yet on his way home through Paris the King found the politicians coolly unresponsive; French bankers were prepared to offer the loan which the Germans had declined to make, but with such tight political strings that Greece would have become almost a French satrapy. The King arrived in Athens, angry with the old Protecting Powers for treating the sovereign of Greece as if he were a dependent client.

The coming of war in 1914 took the Greek royal family by surprise. Most were abroad: Prince George, who lived mainly at St Cloud in France, was at Bernstorff sailing with Prince Waldemar, his close friend and the youngest of his Danish uncles; Prince Nicholas and the widowed Queen Olga were in St Petersburg, so soon to be known at Petrograd; Prince Christopher was visiting his aunt, Queen Alexandra, at Marlborough House in the first days of August and saw how enthusiastically the British people went to war. During these critical weeks, King George V found the time to instruct his most experienced equerry, Sir Frederick Ponsonby, to find a ship which could take the school-age members of the Greek royal family to the neutral Netherlands. The Admiralty placed a destroyer on stand-by alert in case of disaster during the children's voyage to Flushing.

In Athens King Constantine was at once faced with a grave decision. Early on 1 August he received a telegram from the Kaiser asking for Greek entry into the war, partnering Germany and Austria-Hungary 'in a united crusade against Slav domination in the Balkans'. After a day of consultation, the King decided clearly on a policy: Greece would remain strictly neutral so long as the recent settlement in the Balkans was not in danger, he telegraphed back to Berlin. This answer disappointed Wilhelm II; in a marginal note to the telegram, he commented that a neutral Greece,

Constantine I escorts his widowed mother from the palace in Athens to an official function, 1913. She was to spend five years of war and revolution in her native Russia.

pledged to maintain the equilibrium in the Balkans, must be treated as a likely enemy. How long could the Greeks stay out of the war?

Over the following fifteen months that same question was asked with impatient incomprehension in other capital cities, too. Greece was bound by only one treaty obligation: a pledge of aid to Serbia in meeting a Bulgarian attack, provided that the Serbs could concentrate an army of at least 150,000 men against the common Balkan enemy. Bulgaria, however, remained neutral during the 1914 crisis. So, at first, did the Sultan; but when, in October, it became clear that Turkey would soon become Germany's ally, many Greeks wished to assist the Entente Powers, hoping thereby to gain the prize of Constantinople. Venizelos, who was beginning his fifth successive year as prime minister, made offers of intervention which were not authorized by his King. For the moment, Venizelos's private diplomacy remained ineffectual; for, as King Constantine well knew, the Tsar's ministers had no intention of allowing the Greeks to enter Constantinople and become masters of the Straits.

By the middle of January 1915 the British were committed to 'a demonstration of some kind against the Turks', the genesis of the Gallipoli campaign. Churchill, as First Lord of the Admiralty, wished for assistance from the Greek fleet and, perhaps, from a Greek army corps; other allied leaders hoped to establish an allied base at Salonika which could provide aid for Serbia up the valleys of the Vardar and Morava rivers. If the Russians continued to veto a Greek presence at Constantinople, King

Constantine was to be tempted by offers of land elsewhere.

Yet, unlike Venizelos, the King was not attracted by suggestions of territorial gain along the Smyrna-Ephesus coastline, where there were large Greek communities; a foothold on the edge of Anatolia was strategically precarious. 'It would be sheer madness for us to go to Asia Minor,' Prince Nicholas recalls him as saying. He was, however, impressed by what was happening off the Dardanelles, although when the Gallipoli venture unfolded in the spring he argued that the troops should have landed higher up the Gulf of Saros, near Belair, rather than at the tip of the peninsula. Soon the British Minister in Athens could report that King Constantine was prepared to show a 'benevolent neutrality' towards the Entente allies; and in February he authorized the use of Mudros as a British base of operations. Momentarily, early in March, the King even gave reluctant consent to Greek naval and military participation in the campaign. But he found himself faced at once with intense opposition from his friend and military protégé, Joannis Metaxas, the acting Chief of the General Staff. The army was not yet ready to contemplate a long campaign against powerful enemies, Colonel Metaxas argued; and, to back up his convictions, he offered his resignation. So impressed was King Constantine by Metaxas's warnings that he changed his mind over Greek participation in the war. Venizelos, conscious of the deep divergence of opinion between the sovereign and his ministers, gave up the premiership on 6 March. The King invited Dimitrios Gounaris to form a minority government; and the kingdom prepared for a June election.

Before it could be held King Constantine's health gave way. In April he contracted pneumonia and pleurisy; a month later he underwent an operation for the removal of two ribs, only to be weakened still further by an infection of the blood. So grave was his illness that a warship was sent to the Cyclades to bear the miraculous holy ikon of the Virgin and Child from the shrine of Panayia Evanghelistria to the royal sick-room, the first occasion upon which the sacred image had left Tinos. When the ikon was carried to King Constantine's bedside he had already received the last rites; with ebbing strength he venerated the sacred image and lapsed into unconsciousness. That evening he rallied; the ikon remained beside his bed until, a week later, he was out of danger. It was then reverently returned to Tinos, to await the pilgrims who, in 1915 as in every other year, travelled to the island on 15 August for the festival of the Dormition of the Mother of God. Queen Sophie, whose conversion to Orthodoxy provoked the Kaiser to such bitter reproaches twenty-five years before, presented a magnificent sapphire to enrich the ikon as an expression of thanks for her husband's recovery.

The King's illness stilled but did not silence the political controversies around him. Venizelos's liberals won an overall majority in the general election, which was held on 13 June; but ten more weeks elapsed before the King's convalescence was considered sufficiently advanced for him to entrust the formation of a new government to the formidable Cretan. Almost immediately the war crisis intensified. The German and Austrian High Commands decided on swift action to eliminate Serbia and establish through communications between Berlin and Constantinople; they proposed to entice

Bulgaria into the war with promises of territory in Serbian Macedonia. News reached Athens on 23 September that King Ferdinand was mobilizing the Bulgarian army.

That afternoon there was a stormy meeting between King Constantine and Venizelos; the Prime Minister had already invited the British and French to send troops to Salonika in order to aid the Serbs and check a Bulgarian thrust southwards. The King knew nothing of this invitation, and it was only with considerable misgivings that he agreed to call 180,000 reservists to their war stations as a precaution against a Bulgarian attack. Meanwhile the British and French went ahead slowly with preparations for the Salonika expedition: HMS *Scourge* landed a group of senior British and French staff officers on Friday, 1 October; and four days later two transports bringing a British division and a French division from Mudros arrived at the port. On that same Tuesday King Constantine, intensely angered by Venizelos's independent approaches to the Entente allies, dismissed his Prime Minister and appointed Andrew Zaimis as his successor. It was too late to prevent the allied occupation of Salonika.

Despite his indignation at the landings in the second city of his realm, there came a moment in these critical weeks when King Constantine was again tempted to join the Entente allies. In January 1915 King George V had strongly supported a suggestion by his Foreign Secretary, Sir Edward Grey, to 'offer Cyprus to Greece on condition of her joining the Allies', a proposal turned down at that time by the cabinet. With the arrival of allied troops at Salonika, Grey took up the matter again; Britain would cede Cyprus if the Greeks went to the assistance of the Serbs, who were facing an onslaught by German, Austrian and Bulgarian divisions. King Constantine told his brother Prince Nicholas of his reactions: 'When I heard of the proposal, I was carried off my feet with enthusiasm. I would have accepted the offer there and then.' This time, however, the King found both his Prime Minister and the General Staff unwilling to plunge the country into war. The prospect of acquiring Cyprus receded. It is tempting to speculate on what would have happened if the offer had been made to King Constantine nine months earlier, as King George V wished and before the landings at Gallipoli.

The elusiveness of victory at the Dardanelles induced Asquith (Britain's Prime Minister) to send Lord Kitchener (Secretary of State for War) out to Mudros as the winter days closed in. After visiting Gallipoli and Salonika he arrived in Athens on 20 November and was received in audience by King Constantine, who protested at the casual way in which the British and French had breached Greek neutrality. Kitchener, recognizing in the King a fellow soldier forced to work with politicians for whom he felt little respect, was impressed by Constantine's assurances that he did not favour the German cause; and when he returned to England at the end of the month, he showed a greater understanding of the King's concept of neutrality than other members of the cabinet. But by now Kitchener's influence on Asquith and his colleagues was slight. The politicians were obtusely determined not to acknowledge that the King of the Hellenes could be 'pro-Greek' without being 'pro-German'.

The French Government and its emissaries were more hostile to King Constantine than the British. Overall allied command at Salonika had been entrusted to General

Constantine 1, in parade uniform with his marshal's baton, stands on the palace steps with members of the royal family.

Maurice Sarrail, a radical republican free-thinker, the outsider among officers predominantly Catholic and often sentimentally royalist in their sympathies. Sarrail was a courageous soldier who had shown initiative on the Marne in the crucial opening weeks of the war, but his appointment to command 'the Army of the Orient' was essentially a political move designed to keep an alleged crypto-Jacobin away from Paris. He had little respect for any of the crowned heads of Europe and scant regard for the niceties of civil liberty. From the moment he landed at Salonika he wished to proclaim a formal state of siege, but strict orders from Paris held him in check. It was a curious situation. The Greek civil administration continued to function; so even did the German, Austrian, Bulgarian and Turkish consulates in the port. Greek troops were still in the barracks of the town and manning Fort Karaburnu, where a battery of Krupp guns guarded the approach to the port. At the end of September there was a German air raid on Salonika, with one bomb falling near a squadron of Greek cavalry which was commanded by the King's brother, Prince Andrew. Sarrail used the air raid as an excuse for rounding up the enemy consular staff and, at the end of January 1916, mounting a combined operation to secure, peacefully, the transfer of Fort Karaburnu from Greek to French gunners. Sarrail's persistent affronts understandably angered King Constantine: 'I will not be treated as if I were a native chieftain,' he complained to Sir Francis Elliot, Britain's Minister in Athens.

55

A few weeks later Sarrail travelled down from Salonika and met King Constantine, the leading Athenian politicians, and some senior officers. The Greek General Staff, he reported to Paris, 'were and will continue to be pro-German', but even Sarrail recognized that the King wished to remain strictly neutral and avoid incidents. The French authorities were, however, needlessly provocative. Despite protests from General Milne (the British commander) Sarrail took over the administration of Salonika early in June and forbade a torchlit procession in honour of the King's name-day. He also supported an attack by Greek republican insurgents on the royalist barracks in the city. Long before October, when Venizelos arrived in Salonika and set up a 'provisional government' in defiance of the King, General Sarrail was encouraging the recruitment of a Greek 'national army' to fight against the Bulgarians, who had occupied eastern Macedonia.

Subversion was rife, too, in Athens. In the second week of July 1916 workers on the royal estate at Tatoi reported the presence of a strange car moving slowly along isolated tracks and eventually eluding the guards and returning to Athens. King Constantine, Queen Sophie and their younger children were all at Tatoi since the heat was unbearable down in Athens. On Friday morning, 14 July – Bastille Day – observers on the slopes at Kifissia saw plumes of smoke rising from the woodlands, seven miles away. As the summer had been so exceptionally hot, with no rain for five months, it was not surprising that the flames spread rapidly. Soon, however, the observers realized that they were watching not one fire, but several. It was only at great risk that Queen Sophie, carrying the three-year-old Princess Katherine in her arms and with her other children led by calm-headed workers on the estate, succeeded in reaching a road clear of the flames. King Constantine and Prince Christopher (who had gone to his assistance) would have perished had it not been for their familiarity with woodland paths they had known all their lives. The fires burned throughout the weekend: two-thirds of the estate was devastated; a small museum of local antiquities set up by King George and other early buildings were destroyed. Far more tragic, however, was the loss of life: eighteen people were killed, including the King's aide-de-camp Colonel Dellaporta and three chauffeurs, whose bodies were found in their burnt-out cars. It was assumed that the fire had been started deliberately. The identity of the arsonists was never discovered.

Prince Nicholas travelled to Petrograd and to London that summer, to explain and clarify the policies of his royal brother, while Prince Andrew went to Paris and then across the Channel to England. The King could also count on support in Paris from the brother closest to him in age, Prince George, whose wife – Princess Marie Bonaparte – was greatly admired by Aristide Briand, Prime Minister of France from October 1915 to March 1917. Briand was so intimate a friend of 'the Georges' that his biographer, Georges Suarez, recalls how 'in French political circles and the press, Briand ... was suspected of trying to promote the accession to the throne of Prince George of Greece'. This is unlikely: Prince George remembered Venizelos, the Entente's protégé, from his days in Crete and looked upon him as an ambitious rebel; and he was scrupulously loyal to the King, angrily upbraiding the Prime Minister in his

Troops on the move out of Salonika after the French General, Maurice Sarrail, assumes complete military control of the port in June 1916.

own sitting-room when he believed France was humiliating Greece. Princess Marie, who had accompanied her husband to Athens during the King's grave illness, tried to remain both a French patriot and a Greek princess: she established a military hospital in Salonika in November 1915; and she took care to insist in private conversation that, though individual politicians might favour France's enemies, her royal brother-in-law in Athens would never side with his imperial brother-in-law in Berlin.

Both Tsar Nicholas II and King George V were disturbed at the extent to which (in the Tsar's words) 'the Protecting Powers ... are gradually immersing themselves too much in' Greece's 'internal home affairs, to the detriment of the King'. On 4 September George V, in forwarding the Tsar's complaint to Asquith, added his own protest at 'General Sarrail's arbitrary conduct' in 'a neutral and friendly country'. He thought that 'in this Greek question we have allowed France too much to dictate a policy, and that as a Republic she may be somewhat intolerant of, if not anxious to abolish, the monarchy in Greece. But this is *not* the policy of my government.' Recent telegrams from Elliott had suggested that King Constantine might shortly take Greece into the war on the side of the Entente; and King George V commented on this new mood in Athens: 'Public opinion in Greece, as well as the opinion of the King, is evidently changing and if the Allies would treat her kindly and not, if I may say so, in a bullying spirit, she will in all probability join them.'

Unfortunately, the 'bullying spirit' persisted. Even as George V was writing his

57

letter to Asquith, an allied squadron of ten battleships, three cruisers and fifty-seven other warships covered the waters between Salamis and the promontory below Vougliameni. This greatest fleet ever concentrated in the Saronic Gulf was commanded by a Frenchman, Vice-Admiral Dartige du Fournet; but eighteen of the seventy warships flew the White Ensign. Despite amicable meetings between King Constantine and the Vice-Admiral, naval and military pressure was maintained on the government in Athens throughout the last four months of the year. Successive demands led to the seizure of Austrian and German merchant vessels at Eleusis and Piraeus, French supervision of Greek telegraph and postal services, the neutralization of Greek warships at Salamis and Phaleron, and French control of all railway movements around Athens. The King resisted Dartige's request for the handing over of artillery, but he was negotiating the transfer of a battery of mountain guns when, on 1 December, Athenian resentment at the humiliations inflicted by the Entente allies exploded in a tragic incident outside the Zappeion Exhibition Hall.

At eleven o'clock that morning a force of French seamen and British marines came under fire from sharpshooters on Philopappos Hill; fighting continued for much of the day. Dartige du Fournet, who was himself at the Zappeion, signalled to his warships to bombard the area around the Stadium, which seemed the centre of resistance. Sir Francis Elliott and the French emissary were with the King in the royal palace when the naval guns opened fire; Queen Sophie and her younger children spent two hours sheltering in the palace cellars, for the building was hit several times, one shell falling close to the King's study but failing to explode. Over 200 French and British officers and men were killed or wounded that day, and there were heavy casualties among the Greeks, too. Not unreasonably, King Constantine believed that republican extremists had begun the shooting in order to provoke a grave incident; but it is significant that a British major reported that the French were already firing blanks to disperse an angry crowd before the fighting escalated with the fusillade from Philopappos Hill.

These tragic events on 1 December 1916 completed the breach between King Constantine and the Entente Powers. Allied naval mastery established so effective a blockade of Greek ports that for fifteen weeks not a single bushel of wheat was imported into those regions of the country still loyal to the King, an appalling hardship to inflict on a nation so recently described as 'neutral and friendly'. News of the shooting at the Zappeion reached London at a moment of political crisis, during the last days of the Asquith Coalition Government. The succession of Lloyd George to the premiership brought to high office an imaginative Celt whose romantic radicalism was fired by admiration for Venizelos; and King Constantine was treated even less sympathetically than under the Asquith Government. Only the veto of the Tsar prevented the French and British from deposing Constantine; and when, early in March 1917, Nicholas II was forced to abdicate, the King lost his last effective protector. Early in June 1917 the French High Commissioner in Athens, Charles Jonnart, gave the King notice to quit: once he abdicated and left the country the allies would lift the blockade of Greek ports. As the King's eldest son had served in

Montreux, 1920

Above *Princess Helen, with her father, in the sunshine of Montreux.*

Above right *Prince Alexander of Greece (left) with his uncle, Prince Andrew (centre) shortly before Alexander's accession.*

Right *King Alexander, Constantine I's second son, was unexpectedly called to the throne in June 1917 when his father and elder brother were unacceptable to the allied Powers.*

The Dowager Queen Olga at Brindisi on her way back to Athens in October 1920. She was the only member of the royal family permitted to return to Greece during King Alexander's fatal illness, but she did not arrive at Tatoi until a few hours after her grandson's death. Thereafter she was Regent until the return of Constantine I two months later.

the German army during 1911 and 1912 he was unacceptable as a successor. But Jonnart raised no objections to the accession of the second-born Prince Alexander, who was then approaching his twenty-fourth birthday.

King Constantine did not formally abdicate. He told his second son that he should regard the throne as a trust which he held during the absence of his father and elder brother. Jonnart, aware of the deposed King's continued popularity in Athens, insisted that he should leave from a small port rather than sail out into exile from Piraeus. He embarked on the morning of 15 June in the shallow bay of Oropos, sixteen miles east of Tatoi. Fishermen knelt and wept as all the royal family except King Alexander left for Sicily and ultimately for Switzerland. Eventually, a year later, they were joined at St Moritz by Queen Olga, who had remained in her native Russia managing the hospital which she had founded at Pavlovsk until the Bolsheviks made life impossible for her and she was rescued, under Danish diplomatic protection.

Greece's new young ruler had no opportunity to practise the 'democracy under a king' in which his grandfather had believed. Prince Christopher recalls that his nephew was 'a prisoner in his own palace' and adds that 'only the known enemies of his father and of the Royal House were permitted to be in his service', while Princess Alice describes how, on returning as prime minister, Venizelos instantly dismissed her husband 'Prince Andrew, and 3,000 other officers from the Army, for being loyal to the King'. Under these circumstances it would be hardly surprising if the chief interests of King Alexander remained motorcars, pet animals, and his fiancée – Aspasia Manos, the twenty-year-old daughter of Colonel Petros Manos, an equerry of the exiled monarch. But Alexander had been trained as an artilleryman and, despite his resentment at the restraints imposed by the Venizelists, he watched with pride the emergence of his new, French-drilled, army.

Technically Greece declared war on Germany, Austria-Hungary, Turkey and Bulgaria in July 1917, but political schism prevented the army from contributing to the allied cause until the closing months of the long conflict. By May 1918, however, the Greeks could claim a new battle honour in having stormed the Skra di Legen, a heavily fortified Bulgarian position on a mountainous ridge; and by mid-September, when General Franchet d'Espérey launched the offensive in the Moglena Mountains which carried the Allies to final victory, a quarter of a million Greeks were under arms. Many fought with valour alongside the British 22nd Division at Lake Doiran. King Alexander was popular with the British staff officers in Macedonia. During one royal visit to the front, General Milne presented Alexander with an Alsatian dog, taken prisoner a few nights previously by a British patrol: 'Fritz' soon became the young King's inseparable companion.

Greek participation in the final offensive bolstered the territorial claims which Venizelos put forward forcefully at the Paris Peace Conference. He failed to wrest the Dodecanese from Italy, but he argued persuasively in favour of northern Epirus and eastern Thrace, the international control of Constantinople, and the acquisiton of Smyrna and its hinterland. Under protective cover from French, British and American warships, Greek troops landed at Smyrna on 15 May 1919. Although King Alexander paid a brief visit to Paris while the statesmen were making peace, he pursued no active role so long as Venizelos's primacy remained unchallenged. In an unostentatious religious ceremony at Athens on 4 November 1919 he married Aspasia Manos, who never took the title of Queen. The King was in eastern Thrace in July 1920 when his troops occupied Adrianople, but he did not cross to Asia Minor, where Greek troops brushed aside Turkish nationalist opposition, occupied Brussa and reached the Sea of Marmora. When the Sultan accepted the Treaty of Sèvres in the second week of August 1920, it seemed as if King Alexander would, within a few years, become sovereign of a Hellenic kingdom astride the Aegean. There was a resistance movement in central Anatolia, led by General Mustafa Kemal, but in both Paris and Athens politicians and soldiers were not inclined to take seriously so improvised a challenge. In the second week of October Venizelos sought British support for a Greek offensive against Kemal's base at Angora (Ankara), as the next step towards realization of the Great Idea.

Even while Lloyd George's cabinet was discussing Venizelos's proposal, a personal tragedy reached its terrible climax at Tatoi. On 27 September King Alexander, his hands greasy from tinkering with the engine of his car, was returning home with Fritz when the dog was involved in a scrap with two pet monkeys, belonging to the manager of the Tatoi estate. In separating the animals, the King received a bite in the leg from the male monkey. Doctors treated the wound but did not cauterize it. Within hours the wound turned septic. Although she was three months pregnant, Princess Aspasia nursed her husband for four weeks, comforting him through seven operations, before a merciful death came to him on 25 October. Petty political spite denied the exiled Queen Sophie the right to come to her dying son's bedside. But Queen Olga – so recently a scourge to the Bolsheviks – could not be refused entry to the kingdom she had served so loyally. Sadly she reached Tatoi twelve hours after her grandson's death. Five months later, on 25 March 1921, Queen Olga became a great-grandmother; the young king's posthumous daughter was named Alexandra in his honour.

King Alexander's death posed a constitutional problem. Who was to rule the Hellenes? Prince Paul rejected overtures from Venizelos. The regency passed, as of right, to Queen Olga. But it was the Greek people who decided the question of sovereignty. In elections on Sunday, 14 November 1920, they turned against Venizelos, giving the opposition parties 120 more seats than his liberals. On the following Wednesday Venizelos left the country, his ship passing the vessel which was bringing the Princes Andrew and Christopher home. They were welcomed warmly on the quayside and in the capital itself. The monarchist sentiments of the Athenians were beyond question that winter; and on 5 December a plebiscite showed that the Greek people as a whole shared their mood: 1,010,788 votes for King Constantine's restoration, 10,883 votes against. A fortnight later the cruiser *Averoff* brought the much maligned King back to his homeland. He disembarked at Corinth, completing the journey to Athens by train. So excited was the crowd which awaited him at the Peloponnisou Station that people flocked down the railway track itself, preventing the train from pulling into the platform.

The triumphant return was followed by double marriage links which associated Greece with the largest of the Balkan kingdoms, Romania. Crown Prince George married Princess Elisabeth, the eldest daughter of King Ferdinand I, in Bucharest on 27 February 1921; and George's sister, Princess Helen, married Crown Prince Carol of Romania in Athens twelve days later. But for King Constantine these royal nuptials were no more than a happy interlude during weeks of political perplexity. Should he continue the Anatolian adventure which the Venizelists had begun? The army had been mobilized for almost all of the past ten years and he had received clear warnings

Left above Constantine I at Montreux during his first exile, with his brothers, the Princes Nicholas, Andrew and Christopher and his son, Crown Prince George.

Far left Queen Sophie, in mourning for her son Alexander, returns to Greece in December 1920, accompanied by her daughter, Princess Helen.

Left Constantine I acknowledges Athenian cheers from the balcony of the royal palace on his return from exile in December 1920.

George II with his sisters, Queen Helen of Romania and Princess Irene, amid the snows of Switzerland, accompanied by Infante Alfonso and Infanta Beatrice of Spain.

from Paris, Rome and London that he could not count on allied support in the confrontation with Kemalist Turkey. But if he sought a negotiated peace, surrendering the gains promised to Greece in the Treaty of Sèvres, would his political opponents blame him for betraying the Great Idea? Unwisely he decided that the war should go on.

In the last week of May 1921 the King himself set out for Asia Minor to take command of his army. On the eve of his departure he attended a solemn *Te Deum* at the cathedral in Athens. During the long service, with its elaborate ritual, the King was unwell, suffering a haemorrhage where the surgeons had made the incision to remove two ribs when he was ill with pleurisy six years before. Even so he crossed to Smyrna in the second week of June; Prince Andrew, who accompanied his brother, asserts that the King was 'never able to take an active part in the leadership', but he remained in Asia Minor for three months. He returned to Athens at the end of September with his health shattered by the gruelling conditions of a campaign which carried his army as far as the River Sakharia, the last defensive position west of Kemal's capital, Angora (Ankara). Other members of the royal family were also in Asia Minor: Prince Nicholas was at headquarters; Prince Andrew, commanding XII Division, contributed to the victory at Eskisehir on 21 July but was soon disillusioned by the political intrigues and returned to a command in Epirus later in the year; and Crown Prince George brought his young wife to Smyrna. There, at the height of the campaign, the Crown Princess was taken gravely ill and lost the child she was expecting. Neither her health nor her marriage fully recovered from this latest tragedy in what seemed, in these years, a doom-ridden dynasty.

The Greeks were forced back from the Sakharia after a 22-day battle in late August, but retained a firm foothold in Asia Minor for another twelve months. Mounting Turkish confidence frustrated peace talks in the following spring and, in August 1922, the well-equipped Kemalist army was able to mount a new offensive which in ten days inflicted upon King Constantine's weary troops a shattering defeat. On 9 September the first Turkish column entered Smyrna, a city systematically sacked for five days with sickening brutality and thereafter consumed by fire. British and French warships helped rescue survivors but far too few escaped. Prince Paul, who was serving as a sub-lieutenant aboard the cruiser *Elli*, witnessed the first stage of the evacuation, his ship engaging the Turkish shore batteries before finding shelter off Samos. There the Prince learnt that two colonels, Nicholas Plastiras and Stylianos Gonatas, had led an insurrection on Chios and were demanding the abdication of the King.

King Constantine, whose health was failing rapidly, sent for his old friend, Metaxas. Should he defy the colonels and risk civil war? At heart the King knew the answer he must receive. For, staunch royalist though Metaxas remained, the only advice he could offer was immediate abdication so as to prevent bloodshed and save the dynasty. On 27 September the King signed an act of abdication, which Metaxas drafted, and formally proclaimed the accession of Crown Prince George. Once again he sailed away to Italy; but this time he was too ill to travel farther than Sicily. Less than four months later – on 11 January 1923 – King Constantine died in a hotel at Palermo.

Greece was not entirely spared bloodshed. Plastiras, the leader of the colonels, wished to intimidate the new king. Having announced that they were rescinding the royal prerogative of mercy, the revolutionaries put on trial the former prime minister Gounaris, together with the last commander-in-chief in Anatolia and four other politicians. All six men were condemned to death and summarily shot on 28 November. By then, waiting in the cells and himself expecting execution, was Prince Andrew. But King George V, sickened by so many killings in Russia, personally ordered HMS *Calypso* to Piraeus to save his first cousin, while Lord Curzon, the Foreign Secretary, sent a former naval attaché, Captain Gerald Talbot, to negotiate the release of the Prince. The intervention was effective. The Prince was driven straight from his cell to the quayside. *Calypso*, with Princess Alice also aboard, sailed for Corfu, where she embarked Prince Andrew's family: his four daughters; and Prince Philip, who had been born at *Mon Repos*, eighteen months before. 'Delightful' company, the cruiser's captain was to recall: 'They were rather amusing about being exiled, for they so frequently are.'

Queen Marie of Romania with two Greek princesses in Romanian national costume, her daughter-in-law Princess Helen and Princess Irene.

4

THE REIGNS
OF GEORGE II

King George II, thirty-three years old at his accession, was unwilling to become a royal cipher, as Venizelos had sought to make his brother Alexander five years before. So indignant was he at the summary execution of 'the Six' two months after he came to the throne that he wished to go into voluntary exile as a gesture of protest, but he listened to Colonel Metaxas, who urged him to wait at Tatoi until the revolutionaries began to fall out amongst themselves. This was shrewd advice; unfortunately the Colonel himself was too impatient to wait upon events. For the revival of the anti-monarchist Military League in July 1923 prompted Metaxas to organize an attempt to seize power in October, in the hopes of dissolving the Military League and ousting Plastiras, Gonatas and the whole republican coterie of colonels. Metaxas's coup failed; and, though there is no evidence that King George II knew of the conspiracy, it rebounded against the monarchy. Elections in December 1923 returned an overwhelmingly republican parliament. A few days later the King accepted Gonatas's suggestion that it would be as well for him to accompany Queen Elisabeth on an extended visit to her native Romania. During the King's absence parliament passed a decree which established a republic on 25 March 1924, a decision endorsed by plebiscite two and a half weeks later. After fifteen months of political shadow-boxing, distasteful to a soldier of his temperament, King George II was beginning almost twelve years of exile. He never abdicated.

The coming of a Greek republic forced more than twenty descendants of the first King of the Hellenes to seek sanctuary in other lands. The family matriarch, Queen Olga, settled at first in London with her daughter Princess Marie, whose first husband, Grand Duke George Nicolaevitch, was killed by the Bolsheviks. In December 1922 Princess Marie's intensive Greek patriotism encouraged her to marry Captain Pericles Joannides of the cruiser *Elli*, at Wiesbaden, but she spent the following four years caring for her mother. In London, too, was Queen Olga's youngest son, Prince Christopher. In 1920 he had married the widowed American millionairess, Mrs Nancy Leeds, created Princess Anastasia by King Constantine. The Leeds family link with the dynasty was strengthened in 1921 by the marriage of Princess Marie's daughter,

Above *Queen Sophie, in exile at Montreux, with her son, Crown Prince George.*

Left above *Prince Christopher escorts his widowed sister-in-law, Queen Sophie, into the church for his wedding at Palermo, February 1929.*

Left below *George II, with his wife Queen Elisabeth, in Palermo for the wedding of his uncle, Prince Christopher, and Princess Françoise of France, in February 1929. The bridegroom's brother, Prince George, is behind the King, while Prince Paul follows the Queen.*

Xenia, to Prince Christopher's stepson. When Princess Anastasia died in London in 1923 the Prince bought a villa in Rome, which became Queen Olga's final home. She died in Rome in June 1926: her remains were interred in the crypt of the Orthodox Church in Florence, alongside the coffin of her son, Constantine. There, in January 1932, was brought the body of Queen Sophie, who had died from cancer in Frankfurt.

But for several years before her health gave way Queen Sophie lived in Florence, establishing a home with her younger daughters, the Princesses Irene and Katherine, at the Villa Bobolina in the Via Bolognese. The Queen's widowed daughter-in-law Princess Aspasia and her grandchild, Princess Alexandra, were occasional visitors to Florence, although they preferred Venice and the Princess went to school in Sussex. Most other members of the royal family made France their home. Prince George continued to live at St Cloud; there Princess Marie Bonaparte pursued her studies in psychoanalysis with increasing distinction and fired the imaginative perception with which her son, Peter, and her daughter, Eugenie, completed their education. Prince Andrew and his family also settled in St Cloud while Prince and Princess Nicholas, with their two younger daughters, made their home in Paris. The eldest daughter, Princess Olga, married Prince Paul of Yugoslavia in Belgrade in October 1923, but

Two of the three beautiful daughters of Prince and Princess Nicholas, as photographed by Cecil Beaton: **left,** *Princess Olga (born 1903) married Prince Regent Paul of Yugoslavia (1893–1976);* **right,** *Princess Marina (1906–68) married the Duke of Kent (1902–42).*

spent most of the next eleven years abroad; their first child, Prince Alexander, was born at White Lodge, Richmond Park.

King George II gradually drifted apart from Queen Elisabeth, who remained in Romania while her husband spent most of his exile in western Europe, finally settling in London. To England, too, came Prince Paul, after a few months with his mother in Florence. The Prince, calling himself 'Paul Beck', worked for a year as an apprentice aircraft mechanic at Armstrong-Whitworth's factory in Coventry, living for some ten months in Leamington. In the summer of 1930, having grown a flowing beard and assumed yet another false identity, he slipped into Greece as a crewman on a friend's yacht. He was able to show his companions Athens and even his old rooms at Tatoi. Prince Paul remained unmarried so long as he was in exile. George II's marriage was dissolved in July 1935, the King learning of his divorce from the columns of an English newspaper.

During the late 1920s and early 1930s the royal brothers naturally enjoyed the lighter side of English life but, although the King declined to make political statements during his exile, he never became a mere social butterfly, isolated from reality within the comfort of Brown's Hotel. He was the sole luncheon guest of George V on 24 August 1931, that historic Monday when the King-Emperor persuaded the party leaders to form Britain's first coalition in peacetime. King George II was in London, too, on 10 October 1934, attempting to console the dazed eleven-year-old schoolboy who had suddenly become King Peter II of Yugoslavia on the assassination of his father at Marseilles. More happily, seven weeks later he joined other members of his family at Westminster Abbey for the marriage of his first cousin, Princess Marina, to the Duke of Kent, George V's youngest son. 'I am sure we shall like Marina and that she will be a charming addition to the family,' Queen Mary had told her husband when the young couple became engaged in August.

Meanwhile the Greek republic stumbled from crisis to crisis, the life expectancy of any government becoming almost exactly six months, while *coups d'état* took place at an average of one in every forty-two weeks. The most serious abortive uprising, in which Venizelos and General Plastiras were the leading conspirators, took place at the beginning of March 1935, with opposing army units threatening civil war in Thrace and Macedonia, while the cruiser *Elli* fired on rebel destroyers in Kavalla harbour. At last, early in July 1935, the Deputy Prime Minister, General Kondylis – traditionally a republican strongman – announced his conversion to constitutional monarchism on the grounds that it was the only system which could combat spiritual anarchy and ensure respect for the state. Kondylis assumed the premiership himself early in October, encouraged the National Assembly to declare in favour of a restoration of the monarchy, and prepared for a plebiscite to be held on 3 November.

When it was announced that 1,491,992 votes had been cast for a restoration and

A Balkan conference: George II (left) with Alexander of Yugoslavia. Both kings married daughters of Ferdinand I of Romania, the Princesses Elisabeth and Marie.

Left *George II with two young kinsmen, his nephew, Prince Michael of Romania, and his fair-haired cousin, Prince Philip (c. 1926).*

Below *George II pays a courtesy call on the French President at the Elysée Palace.*

only 32,454 against, General Kondylis is reported by Lincoln MacVeagh, the US Minister, to have 'expressed annoyance with his supporters for "exaggerating"'. Yet, although the decisiveness of the figures caused raised eyebrows among sceptical diplomats, the result genuinely reflected the mood of revulsion with republicanism inside Greece. King George and Crown Prince Paul crossed from Brindisi to Old Phaleron in the *Elli* on 25 November: bands, bunting and pealing church bells greeted them but, as MacVeagh noted, the 'popular rejoicing' was more restrained than at the time of King Constantine's return. The British, American and German Ministers were all, at first, unimpressed by the King's personality, complaining, rather curiously, of his 'listless attitude' and his 'languid' return of military salutes. But within a few weeks the British and Americans had changed their minds: Sir Sydney Waterlow, the British Minister, commented on the good fortune of the Greeks in having at this critical time a ruler who was impartial, averse to totalitarianism, and yet strong-minded; and by the end of February 1936 MacVeagh could write a long personal letter to his friend, President Roosevelt, in which he praised the King as 'a serious-minded and genuine person determined to do his best as Monarch of the entire country and not simply of one party'. MacVeagh, a boyhood companion of F.D.R., later became more critical of George II as a national leader, but he never ceased to admire his sense of duty and during the Second World War he fostered a valuable friendship between monarch and president.

In his first message to 'the Hellenes' King George courageously reminded them of the dynasty's motto, 'My Strength is the Love of My People'. For nine months he tried to re-charge the political machine, ridding himself of kingmaker Kondylis when the General objected to the total and unconditional amnesty he proclaimed to his subjects. But the great influx of refugees from Asia Minor had increased the political strength of the extreme left and by the summer of 1936 the fifteen communist deputies enjoyed considerable bargaining power between the royalist and republican blocks in parliament, which were numerically almost equal. An unexpectedly high mortality rate among experienced politicians induced the King to appoint General Metaxas as prime minister, the communist party (KKE) responding with a call for a general strike to begin on Wednesday, 5 August. But Metaxas moved first: on the Tuesday the king authorized his prime minister to set up a temporary dictatorship so as to combat the emergency. Soon Metaxas had purloined the trappings of a Fascist state, and much of its ideology, too. But whereas self-made ex-corporals in other lands would strut about in popinjay uniforms, General Metaxas – a first-rate soldier from the old Cephalonian aristocracy – liked to show he was one of the people by invariably wearing civilian clothes.

'I understand that M. Metaxas makes 500 enemies a day – and on some days 5,000,' the French Minister remarked ten weeks after the setting up of the dictatorship. Would Metaxas fall before the winter was over and bring the monarchy crashing down with him, foreign observers wondered? King George was alive to the danger, but he was confident that he could handle Metaxas as adroitly as he had handled Kondylis. More than once he emphasized to Sir Sydney Waterlow that the 'Fourth

73

The restoration of the monarchy, 1936; a smiling George II is followed ashore by Prince and Princess Christopher, by his sisters, Princess Irene and Queen Helen, and by his brother, Crown Prince Paul.

of August' regime was a passing phenomenon, an emergency government to deal with the communist menace in Salonika, Kavalla and Piraeus; as for the General himself, 'The idea has always been that he should retire when he has done his work,' Waterlow reported George II as saying. But some of the King's closest relatives were uneasy. Crown Prince Paul, nominally Chief Scout of Greece since 1919, mistrusted the proposed Youth Movement (EON). Others resented press censorship, Prince George returning angrily to France after six months of Metaxas.

Yet, despite warnings from leading liberals that 'we are being dragged to a precipice overhanging the abyss', there was one moment of national unity when the royal family, the Prime Minister and thousands in the streets of Athens came together in homage to the dynasty. On Wednesday, 17 November 1936, the cruiser *Averoff*, flying once more King Constantine's personal standard, reached Piraeus from Brindisi bringing the coffins of the king and his wife and mother from their resting-place at Florence. A solemn procession of eighty white-bearded church dignitaries intoned the prayers for the dead in the cathedral at Athens, and for six days the crowds filed past the catafalques before, on the following Wednesday, they were taken to the mausoleum among the tall pines on the slopes above Tatoi.

King George maintained close links with Britain. Soon after the start of the dictatorship he welcome Edward VIII (and Mrs Simpson) during their cruise in the *Nahlin*, and he travelled to London on private visits in November 1937 and late October 1938, staying for more than seven weeks on the second occasion. His friendship with the lady whom the US Minister calls 'Miss Brown' may have encouraged the King to linger in London, but he also found the time to hold informal talks with cabinet ministers and the paladins of the Foreign Office. Occasionally British diplomats failed to detect the irony in George II's more sardonic observations, as when Waterlow solemnly reported a conversation in Athens which ended with the King remarking that 'the only one real solution ... is that Greece should be taken over by your civil service and run as a British colony'. But the King's sensitivity to British policies was genuine: quite apart from sentimental links, he remembered that Greece was a maritime nation, dependent on imports of food and with a growing mercantile fleet which benefited from the British carrying trade and was insured in London. Not that either he or Metaxas could forget that almost a third of Greece's foreign trade in these years was with Germany, a far higher proportion than with any other country. There were sound reasons why King George sought to perfect 'that attitude of Mr Facing-Both-Ways' which MacVeagh was to analyse so shrewdly in his letters back to Washington.

His surviving brother was almost as much at home in the German-speaking lands as in England. For a few weeks in 1918 Prince Paul had trained as a naval cadet at Kiel, an unprofitable experience dominated by the onrush of mutiny and 'Spanish' influenza. In 1936 he visited Berlin for the XIth Olympiad; there he proposed marriage to his first cousin once-removed, Princess Frederica of Hanover, Duchess of Brunswick-Luneburg, whom he had met several times in her childhood and as a young woman when he visited his sisters in Italy. The Princess, who had only recently celebrated her nineteenth birthday, hesitated over the engagement but by the following summer she had made up her mind, and the Crown Prince was invited to the Duke of Brunswick's Austrian home, Schloss Hubertihaus. Their betrothal was officially announced on 28 September 1937 and the wedding celebrated on 9 January 1938 at the Metropolitan Cathedral in Athens, where another German-born Princess, the future Queen Sophie, was married almost half a century before.

'From this historic moment Greeks will vie with each other for love of you,' Mayor Kotzias of Athens affirmed, with characteristic exuberance, as Princess Frederica stepped down from the train wearing a blue velvet dress and a white fur hat, for even in mid-winter she wished to appear in Greek colours. The state landau, last used in 1889, was refurbished for the wedding itself. Drawn by six white horses, it brought a fairy-tale touch of pageantry to the bride's journey to and from the cathedral, rousing the crowd to cheers and clapping, despite the steady drizzle of a grey winter's day. There followed a cavalcade of twenty royal cars with guests from Britain, Germany, Denmark, Yugoslavia, and Romania, as well as survivors from Tsarist Russia. The jewelled vestments, crowns and croziers of forty church dignitaries in attendance on Archbishop Chrysostomos enriched the marriage service with the unhurried time-lessness of Orthodoxy. 'The singing', MacVeagh noted, was 'something to be remembered for a lifetime.'

Princess Frederica's mother, Princess Victoria, Duchess of Brunswick, was the only daughter of Kaiser Wilhelm II, who followed reports of the wedding festivities with great interest from Huis Doorn, his exiled home in the Netherlands (where the bridal couple were to visit him in February). But, despite these links with Royal Prussia,

The arrival at Piraeus of the coffins of Constantine I, Queen Olga and Queen Sophie for reburial at Tatoi, November 1936. They were buried at Florence during the Republic.

care was taken in Athens to emphasize Princess Frederica's connection with the British monarchy. Had disaster swept away thirty-three prior claimants to the throne the Princess would have been Queen of England, and it was therefore thought expedient for King George VI to summon a Privy Council at which, in accordance with the Royal Marriages Act of 1722, he gave his consent to the wedding. The Duke of Kent was the principal guest from England and the British Legation organized a banquet on the night after the wedding. No special celebrations were organized by the German Legation. The subsequent descent on Athens in rapid succession of three top-ranking Nazis – Goering, Goebbels, Schacht – failed to recover for Germany the propaganda advantage which Anglophiles gained through the royal marriage.

The Crown Prince's wedding was the last parade occasion of the older generation of royal princes. The most senior of them 'Uncle Jakob' – as both bride and bridegroom called Prince George – was to share the later vicissitudes of the monarchy. Prince Nicholas, however, died a month later. Prince and Princess Andrew drifted apart: he settled in Monte Carlo, where he died from a heart attack in December 1944; and his wife Alice, sister of Lord Louis Mountbatten, lived in Athens from 1938 onwards, devoting herself to charitable work in pursuance of the religious vocation which she experienced intensely. Soon Prince Andrew's sister, Princess Marie, was to return to the homeland she passionately loved, having so offended Mussolini by her intensive Greek patriotism that she was expelled from Italy. Her youngest brother Prince Christopher – who had married Princess Françoise of France in 1929 – was living in Rome when his son Prince Michael was born in January 1939, but returned to Athens shortly before his death twelve months later.

The wedding of Princess Frederica to Crown Prince Paul, Athens, 9 January 1938. From left: Duke Ernest Augustus of Hanover (bride's father); Princess Frederica; Prince Paul; the Duchess of Hanover (only daughter of Kaiser Wilhelm II); George II.

During their early married life the Crown Prince and Princess lived in a compact villa at Psychiko, the garden suburb north of Athens. Their daughter, named Princess Sophia after her grandmother, was born there on 2 November 1938; and exactly nineteen months later – on 2 June 1940 – Princess Frederica gave birth there to a son. As Greek churches were on that Sunday celebrating the festival of the 'Thirteenth Apostle', St Constantine the Great, there was never much doubt that the new prince, like his royal grandfather, would bear the name of the first emperor to profess Christianity at Byzantium.

When the Sunday siesta was broken by a salute of 101 guns echoing across the city, some Athenians assumed that war had come suddenly to Greece. For that weekend saw the completion of the Dunkirk evacuation and, with a growing realization of the magnitude of Germany's 'triumph in the West', everyone anticipated that Hitler's Italian ally would speedily seek a compensatory victory on the cheap. In July 1939 King George's sister Princess Irene – for three years Greece's 'First Lady' – married HRH Prince Aimone, Duke of Spoleto in Florence, but this dynastic link did nothing to improve relations between Italy and Greece, which had become strained a few weeks earlier with Mussolini's annexation of Albania. A long press campaign in Rome against the Greeks was followed on 15 August 1940 by the sinking of the *Elli* by an Italian submarine as the cruiser lay off Tinos, protecting thousands of pilgrims, who had come to the holy island for the festival of the Dormition. Metaxas, however unpopular he may have become with the mass of the population, had at least increased the efficiency and effectiveness of the army and navy. When, at three o'clock on the morning of 28 October, Metaxas was awakened at his home in Kifissia by the Italian Minister with a three-hour ultimatum, he was able to reply 'No' with every confidence that the armed services would prevent Mussolini's troops from occupying the strategic points he demanded. Yet neither Metaxas nor King George could foresee the indomitable spirit with which Greek troops thrust the invaders out of Epirus and penetrated deeply into the mountain fastness of Albania.

The King, as Supreme Commander, remained in Athens; almost every day he presided over meetings of the War Council in the Hotel Grande Bretagne. Crown Prince Paul frequently went forward to the front line in the mountains, his wife helping to organize warm clothing and comforts for the troops. When, early in December, there was stalemate in Albania, the British wished to land an expeditionary force at Piraeus or Salonika, a proposal which made both King George and Metaxas uneasy, for fear that it would provoke a German attack. The war brought out Metaxas's finest qualities, but the strain was too great for his health. He died early on 29 January 1941, after a week confined to his home. The loss of Greece's 'strong man' – the first dictator in whose honour flags in London flew at half-mast – left a political void for, like so many domineering personalities in government, he had

Right above George II joins Prince Regent Paul of Yugoslavia and the Duke of Kent at Crown Prince Paul's wedding in January 1938.

Right Prince Christopher on the Acropolis with his wife, Princess Françoise, and his nieces, Queen Helen of Romania and the Princesses Irene and Katherine.

surrounded himself with nonentities; all were anti-Italian, but some still sympathetically inclined towards Nazi Germany. King George himself attempted to give the wartime leadership which the nation required, although he entrusted day-to-day administration to the prominent banker, Alexander Korizis. The King was a courageous soldier of steady nerves, but he lacked charisma and did not inspire deep affection among his people. There were grave misunderstandings within the Greek High Command and between the King, his ministers and a high-level British delegation, which was headed by the Foreign Secretary (Eden), the Chief of the Imperial General Staff (Dill) and the C-in-C Middle East (Wavell). When the Germans, with Bulgarian support, came to the aid of their Italian allies on 6 April 1941, crack units of the Greek army were cut off in western Thrace while the small expeditionary force from the British Commonwealth found the defensive positions which its commanders had expected to hold along the River Aliakmon inadequately prepared. Salonika was in German hands within three days. From 12 April onwards the allies were in retreat, soon falling back behind the pre-1881 frontier.

At ten o'clock at night on the first Sunday of the German attack, a terrible explosion devastated a large area in Piraeus and shook homes as far distant as Tatoi. The ss *Glen Fraser*, with 250 tons of TNT in her hold, had been damaged in an air raid earlier in the evening. Now, when all seemed quiet, she went up in flames, the blast firing two other munition ships moored close by. Next morning King George and Crown Prince Paul hurried to Piraeus hoping that their presence would bolster morale and expedite relief work. As early as Wednesday (9 April) there was talk in Athens of withdrawing the Government to Crete. But on Friday evening King George personally put forward a different proposal to the British Minister: since Crete was vulnerable to air attack, the King and Government, together with 50,000 recruits training in the Peloponnese, should be evacuated to Cyprus, ready to mount a counter-attack against Italian positions in the Dodecanese. This enterprising royal strategic initiative was at once telegraphed to London, where Eden at first treated it favourably. But, after objections from the Colonial Office and from diplomats susceptible to Turkish opinion, the British prevaricated, neither accepting nor flatly rejecting the proposal.

On the following Friday (18 April) Prime Minister Korizis committed suicide; and over the weekend – the Greek Orthodox Easter – King George personally presided over the Government before persuading another banker, Emmanuel Psouderos, to accept the premiership on Monday afternoon. Early on Tuesday morning Crown Princess Frederica, with her two children, Prince and Princess George (who had travelled to Athens in February rather than remain in German-occupied Paris) and the Princesses Katherine, Aspasia and Alexandra, who had been helping in the hospitals for much of the previous week, assembled at Scaramanga in the bay of Eleusis and were evacuated to Crete in a Sunderland flying boat. King George, Crown Prince Paul and the government ministers followed them by a similar route some twenty-four hours later, the unlucky King having to leave Greece on his name-day, Wednesday, 23 April. German troops entered Athens on the following Sunday morning.

The christening of Princess Irene in South Africa, 1942. Back row, from left: Prince Dominik Radziwill, Prince George, Prince Paul, General Smuts holding Princess Irene. Middle row: Mrs Smuts, Princess Katherine, Princess Frederica, Princess Marie. Front row: Princess Tatiana Radziwill (now Madame Fruchaud), Princess Sophia, Prince Constantine.

King George had warned the British that Crete was vulnerable to air attack, and he was right. Crown Princess Frederica described in a letter soon afterwards how there had been an air raid as the royal refugees disembarked from the flying boat at Soudha, forcing them to huddle in a slip trench. 'A Bonaparte mustn't be afraid of cannon,' Princess Marie had been told as a child of eight when a starting gun at Dieppe regatta made her flinch. Now, more than fifty years later, she set a fine example of fortitude during the assault on the island which her husband, Prince George, was convinced he still knew so well. After a week of privation and discomfort the royal evacuees were flown to Alexandria.

Meanwhile the King sought to remain in Crete, having set up headquarters in Khania. With him, as a personal aide-de-camp, was his cousin, Prince Peter of Greece, the only son of Prince and Princess George. So bad was the bombing, however, that the King was forced to move from one house to another, pursued so relentlessly by the Luftwaffe that it seemed as if there must be a formidable fifth column around him. The combined resistance of Greek and British Commonwealth troops almost frustrated the German airborne assault but, as May drew to a close, the allied commander, General Freyberg VC, prepared to evacuate the island. The only chance of escape to Egypt necessitated a gruelling march around the hump of the White Mountain to the southern coast. King George made the journey with a detachment of New Zealanders, travelling sometimes on mules, but having to pick their way so cautiously down the steep-sided gorges that it took three days and nights to reach the coast. Often they came under enemy attack, narrowly escaping capture by parachutists. At last – on 1 June – the King's party was located at Khora Sfakion, where there was a small harbour, and the destroyer HMS *Decoy* was able to take him to join the Greek community living in Egypt. For his leadership under enemy fire in Crete King George II had the unique experience for a reigning sovereign of receiving the DSO, the principal British decoration for distinguished service in the field of battle.

Crown Princess Frederica and her children made Cape Town their wartime home. With them in South Africa were most of the royal party who had shared their misfortunes at Soudha. All had yet another anxious night when fire broke out in a wing of the Government Guest House at which they were staying, but the Prime Minister General Smuts took them into his own home, Groote Schuur. The Crown Princess's third child, Princess Irene, was born at Cape Town in May 1942, and Smuts was a godfather. By then some of the royal ladies had gone to England, notably King Alexander's widow Princess Aspasia and their daughter Princess Alexandra, who met there the exiled King Peter II of Yugoslavia. The two were married in March, 1944 in Upper Grosvenor Street, London. King George II and Crown Prince Paul spent only a short time in South Africa; they established offices for the government-in-exile in London but travelled frequently to Egypt over the following years. The Crown Princess and her children left South Africa for Cairo in February 1944.

By then the whole future of the monarchy was in question. In the immediate aftermath of defeat, even while George II was in the Cretan mountains, Lincoln MacVeagh found among his Athenian acquaintances a mood of lingering resentment which made the King a scapegoat for military failure. Genuinely royalist army officers were, for the most part, serving overseas helping to train Greek brigades for service in North Africa and Italy. When therefore, in the summer of 1942, a powerful resistance movement developed in mainland Greece, it was led by ex-Venizelists (still smarting from their treatment in the Metaxas era), by patriotic Greeks further to the left, or by convinced communists who wished to impose the Soviet system on their compatriots. In early October 1942 British officers, parachuted into the Roumeli Mountains to prepare for the operation which destroyed the Gorgopotamos railway viaduct a month later, found little monarchist sentiment among their Greek companions. Over the following thirty months the Military Mission – originally commanded by Brigadier Myers and, from August 1943, by Colonel Woodhouse (later a Conservative MP for eleven years) – sought not only to unify resistance against the invader, but to prevent the formidable ELAS army from replacing the Hellenic kingdom with a communist republic. That was, of course, also the main objective of

82

George II with British soldiers in Egypt during the Second World War.

King George II and his governments. Over the methods and timing by which this objective would be ensured there remained, however, deep disagreement and often a mutual suspicion.

Churchill, who greatly admired the King's courage and conduct in 1941, was predisposed to support the monarchist cause. His principal lieutenants, Anthony Eden (Foreign Secretary) and Harold Macmillan ('Minister resident at Allied Head-quarters') always retained the deep impressions which their shocked minds received as junior officers during the First World War, when the English press was so hostile to the Greek dynasty. They therefore had less patience with King George II, as their respective memoirs clearly show. Macmillan, in particular, was to criticize him for failing to declare as early as 'the winter of 1943 ... that he would not return until called by a vote of the people'. But the King, unlike his neighbouring royal exile from Yugoslavia, had a deep and bitter experience upon which to draw; his commitments remained guarded, especially after a deputation of resistance leaders was flown to Egypt to meet him in the summer of 1943, and his authority and prestige were weakened by two mutinies among Greek army units in the Middle East and a more serious naval mutiny in Alexandria harbour. Nevertheless he was prepared to make promises on future policy which he knew he could keep: in July 1943 he undertook to authorize elections to a constituent assembly within six months of his restoration; four months later he declared, a shade ambiguously, that 'when the hour of liberation struck, he would examine anew the date of his return'. But, alarmingly, the pace of events quickened in March 1944 when the communists sponsored a Political Committee of National Liberation (PEEA) in the mountains, thereby creating an ELAS-backed alternative 'government'.

The imminence of civil war made King George II wish to land in Greece as soon as possible, while Crown Prince Paul on more than one occasion suggested that he should return aboard a Greek warship as regent and prepare the way for his brother's restoration. But the King continued to move cautiously. In May 1944 he backed the efforts of George Papandreou, an anti-communist ex-Venizelist recently smuggled out of Greece, to meet representatives of all opinions at a conference in the Lebanon where a compromise settlement was reached on the formation by Papandreou of a government of national unity. The King, however, gained the impression from reports of the Lebanon Conference that 'only the extreme Leftists' among the delegates were opposed to 'his returning to Greece before the plebiscite'. Churchill and Macmillan hoped that the British military authorities would be able to supervise the orderly liberation of Greece when the Germans fell back. The Caserta Agreement of September 1944, negotiated primarily between Macmillan and Papandreou, effectively put Lieutenant-General Donald Scobie in command of all the military forces in Greece. Scobie's troops landed at Patras on 4 October 1944 and entered Athens ten days later, the Germans pulling out of mainland Greece over the following three weeks. By the end of the third week in October Papandreou's government was in Greece itself. But, in accordance with allied policy, not the King.

Nor indeed was there any constitutional authority exercising sovereignty in his name. Seven months earlier Prime Minister Psouderos had advised the King to nominate Archbishop Damaskinos, the Primate of Greece, as regent of the kingdom. But King George was resolutely opposed to such an appointment then and nothing would change his opinion, not even backing for the proposal from President Roosevelt. The King regarded Damaskinos as politically ambitious; and he remained convinced – justifiably – that the assumption of a regency by a national figure outside the royal family would diminish the chances of a restoration – had not the Hungarian Regent, Admiral Horthy, refused to allow Hungary's King to remain in Budapest when in 1921 he returned to claim his realm?

Field Marshal Smuts warmly supported King George's stand and told Churchill that he thought the King should land in Greece 'to discharge his proper constitutional functions' as soon as Scobie's troops had broken the strength of the communists. But when would that be? On the first Sunday in December grim street-fighting broke out in Athens between ELAS units and Scobie's inter-allied force. So grave was the civil war that Churchill and Eden flew out to Athens themselves on Christmas Day and sought to mediate, summoning an all-party conference under the chairmanship of Archbishop Damaskinos, whom Churchill met for the first time aboard HMS *Ajax*. It was a curious situation: the Prime Minister of Great Britain, and two of his successors, speeding along the road from Phaleron in armoured cars, while the King of the Hellenes, with a reluctant sense of frustration, spent the last Christmas of the war in

George II and the Crown Prince and Princess drive from Phaleron into Athens, 28 September 1946, on their return from wartime exile.

a London which was under V2-rocket attacks.

Despite the conference, the communist rising in Athens continued for another three weeks, until ELAS accepted a face-saving agreement at Varkiza which brought an uneasy peace to the capital. More immediate was the effect of his 'Greek reconnaissance' on Churchill, for he returned to London convinced that the kingdom needed a regent urgently. At Downing Street, during two long sessions on the night of 29–30 December, he cajoled the King into appointing Archbishop Damaskinos as regent. At the same time the King re-affirmed his desire for the 'processes of democratic government' to ascertain 'the freely expressed wishes of the Greek people as soon as these storms have passed'.

For another fifteen months 'the storms' persisted, rumbling on for almost a year after the fall of Nazi Germany. At last, on 31 March 1946, the first general election in Greece for ten years took place in the presence of British, American and French observers. It brought victory to the predominantly royalist populist bloc, which won 231 of the 354 parliamentary seats. The people of Greece recognized that a constitutional monarchy blessed by the Orthodox Church was the steadiest bulwark against communism. On 1 September, in a high poll which was again scrutinized by

George II addresses Parliament on returning from exile in 1946.

the Americans and British, 69 per cent of the electors voted in favour of the immediate return of King George II. He flew out from London to Eleusis on 27 September.

As in November 1935, the King made his formal return in a warship, joining the Crown Prince and Princess (who had come directly from Alexandria) aboard the destroyer *Miaoulis* off Eleusis. On the morning of 28 September the *Miaoulis* and three escorting vessels entered Phaleron Bay, and from the quayside the royal party went in an open car to the cathedral for a service of thanksgiving. A fortnight later the Crown Princess sailed again for Alexandria and brought her three children back to Athens by sea on 18 October. The Crown Prince and his family were able to live once more in their villa at Psychiko. But, to his great disappointment, King George found that Tatoi, which had been extensively redeveloped in 1937, was again uninhabitable; it had been used as headquarters by a guerrilla band and then in August 1945 ravaged by another fire, started by communists.

With guerrilla warfare still rampant in the mountains, King George was forced to spend most of the winter of 1946–7 in Athens, at the palace in Herodes Atticus Street. In February 1947 he had the satisfaction of formally becoming ruler of the Dodecanese Islands, ceded by Italy to Greece in the Paris Peace Treaties. A month later it was with relief that he read President Truman's message to Congress, pledging military and economic aid to countries threatened by communism and specifically mentioning Greece and Turkey. But, even though the King was only in his mid-fifties, the burdens

The 6-year-old Crown Prince Constantine walks with his father, King Paul, at George II's funeral, April 1947.

of world war, insurrection and political in-fighting had severely weakened his health. Increasingly his brother had to deputize for him in ceremonies away from Athens and, less than five months after his return, he was complaining of giddiness and chest pains.

King George retained a deep sense of duty. On Tuesday, 25 March, he spent two hours taking the salute at the annual Independence Day parade. By the following Sunday he felt exhausted, but on Monday evening he attended a charity performance of the Laurence Olivier film of *Henry V*, given to support Greece's orphaned children. Next morning (1 April) he completed plans to visit Patras and Missolonghi the following weekend. It was a journey he never made. He wanted no lunch that day, but retired to a drawing-room to rest. Shortly before two o'clock he suffered a coronary thrombosis and died.

There is no coronation ceremony in Greece. But the tradition of continuity in kingship is as strong as in western and northern Europe. At eight o'clock that evening the representative of the Ecumenical Patriarch of Constantinople administered the oath of sovereignty to King Paul in the throne room. Four days later the people of Athens became poignantly aware that another reign had begun. As the funeral cortège moved slowly through the capital, they could see, behind the royal bodyguard of evzones, the tall figure of their new sovereign. Holding the King's left hand and keeping carefully in step marched their new Diadoch, the six-year-old Prince Constantine; the top of his head was no higher than his father's elbow.

King Paul and Queen Frederica with the young Princesses Sophia and Irene visiting the village of Avgerinos, Macedonia. Queen Frederica was particularly concerned with the reconstruction of churches and schools in villages destroyed during the civil war.

5

THE HAPPY PARTNERSHIP
KING PAUL AND
QUEEN FREDERICA

With the accession of King Paul the character of the monarchy changed, at first almost imperceptibly. For a third of a century political exigency had tarnished the image of a *vasilevoméni dimokratia*, the 'democracy under a king', which George I sought to perfect before the Balkan Wars. Now there came to the throne a family man who – like the founder of the dynasty – was a naval officer by training rather than a soldier, although in 1940–41 he had seen for himself the impact of modern war on land and in the skies. The new King possessed the double advantages of wide experience in the world outside Greece and also a contented domestic life, with a Queen not quite thirty at his accession and a son and two daughters all under ten. He had not suffered as deeply as his brother from the dynastic humiliations of the First World War and its aftermath. Rather than allow the past to weigh suspiciously on his mind, King Paul looked forwards with an optimism which, in 1947–8, a monarch of less happy disposition would have found difficult to sustain.

The communist insurrection, which had led to fighting in northern Greece in the spring of 1946 and in the mountains of the Peloponnese six months later, became a full-scale civil war soon after King Paul's accession. A new method of terrorizing Greek families into unwilling support for the communists was the threat of abducting children, who would be raised as ideologically sound Marxists across the frontier, in Yugoslavia, Bulgaria or Albania. When the King and Queen visited northern Greece at midsummer 1947, able to move only cautiously in heavily protected convoys, they travelled through a destitute countryside where the villages were menaced by guerrillas as terrible as any bandit raiders during the years of Ottoman misrule. In the first week of July Queen Frederica made a broadcast from Athens, appealing for support for a Northern Provinces Welfare Fund, a charity for which she cared deeply throughout her husband's reign. Chief beneficiaries were orphans and families threatened with abductions: by the end of the year fifty-two children's communities (*Paidoupolis*) were set up under the auspices of the Queen's fund.

King Paul and Prince George visit soldiers in the Greek barracks, Easter 1950.

Six months after his accession King Paul was seriously ill with typhoid fever. He could not attend the wedding of his first cousin, Prince Philip (son of Prince Andrew of Greece), to HRH Princess Elizabeth of Great Britain in London, nor could he make visits to Epirus, where his army had to withstand sustained assaults by the communists on the historic town of Konitsa, which was bombarded from the surrounding heights throughout Christmas week. Not until the end of January 1948 was the King able to resume his normal duties; in his absence Queen Frederica deputized for him. Her commitments during these weeks are testimony both to her sense of service and to two contrasting obligations of modern monarchy – the ceremonially representative and the militarily protective. Thus on 20 November 1947 Queen Frederica was at Westminster Abbey for the royal wedding and next evening at Claridge's Hotel for a dinner at which Churchill, Smuts, and Eden were among the guests; but, as soon as the route was opened up in Epirus in early January, she was in the war zone, travelling on mule-back into shell-shocked Konitsa, despite the danger of land mines and mortar attack. The High Command persuaded King Paul to confer upon his wife a Military Cross for her courage. It was a fitting award for a direct descendant of Prussia's royal heroine, Queen Louise, to receive.

The civil war effectively ended in the last week of August 1949 with a victory of the national army in the Grammos and Vitsi mountains along the Albanian frontier. Despite the moving accounts of the eye-witnesses who reported the conflict, it has never been appreciated outside Greece that the material and psychological effect of the three-year agony on the mainland communities was more disastrous than the Second World War itself. On 14 September King Paul broadcast to his people, making a sombre appeal for help in the reconstruction of 7,000 villages totally destroyed in the fighting; with the damage to towns like Florina, Karpenision, Naousa and Konitsa, this devastation meant that one-tenth of the whole population of Greece had been left homeless by the war.

In a nation which only gave women the vote for the first time in 1952 the forceful intervention of Queen Frederica on behalf of unfortunates victimized once the communist wave receded led to complaints that she was 'meddling in politics'. But, undeterred by her critics, the Queen and her husband persisted in their policy of seeking to assuage lingering bitterness by acts of compassionate reconciliation which individual ministers, military personnel and officials all too rarely emulated. In August 1953 the first of a series of Greek earthquakes wrecked Zakinthos, with Volos and Santorini similarly shaken over the following two years. On each occasion, King Paul and Queen Frederica identified themselves with the stricken victims of disaster, travelling to the devastated areas and seeking not only to comfort the shocked victims, but to cut bureaucratic red tape so as to speed the task of reconstruction. By the mid-1950s their courage and far-sightedness had raised the popularity of the royal family to a new level in Greece.

From 1948 onwards the King had an additional supra-national responsibility. For after his cousin King Michael of Romania was forced to abdicate in December 1947, King Paul was the only remaining Orthodox sovereign in the world, since Russia, Bulgaria and Yugoslavia had already become secular republics. His state visit to Turkey in 1952 therefore gained a double significance: it was the first occasion upon which any head of a Turkish state entertained a Greek sovereign, and the King of the Hellenes dutifully laid a wreath on the tomb of Kemal Ataturk (the father of modern Turkey) in Ankara; but the visit also enabled King Paul to land at Istanbul and meet the Ecumenical Patriarch of Constantinople, a dignitary whose authority within Greece was restricted to the twenty monastic communities on Mount Athos, but who remained the senior primate of Orthodoxy. King Paul himself was a deeply meditative Christian who, in thought-provoking addresses to the universities of Athens and Salonika, sought to stress the interdependence of religion and modern science. In religion, the King hoped to promote unity, tolerance and understanding, as he did in many other areas. But he could not keep in check the passionate nationalistic feelings of others. Within three years of his visit to Istanbul, sixty of the city's eighty Orthodox churches were gutted or sacked by rioting Turks in a single night of fury

Left *Shortly before his 84th birthday Prince George, accompanied by his wife, represented the Greek dynasty at the coronation of Queen Elizabeth II in June 1953. He wears the robes of a Knight of the Order of the Bath and the Danish Order of the Elephant, of which he was a Knight.*

Below *President Eisenhower in Athens with the royal family in 1960.*

at the Greek Cypriots' campaign for union with their Hellenic compatriots.

When King Michael left Romania he was already engaged to marry Princess Anne of Bourbon-Parma. As Bucharest was barred to him, the wedding took place in Athens in June 1948, with Tatoi hurriedly made habitable for the honeymoon and with his mother – King Paul's sister, Queen Helen – coming back to her homeland from exile in Florence for the festivities. Also at the wedding was Prince George, 'Uncle Jakob', who in the following summer celebrated his eightieth birthday in Denmark but would still come with his wife to winter each year at Athens. Yet the royal family circle was smaller than in George II's reign. The King's youngest sister, Princess Katherine, had married Major Richard Brandram in Athens in April 1947 and, after living for some time in Iraq, settled in England, where the Greek Princess was accorded the rank of a British duke's daughter. Princess Alice, the widow of Prince Andrew, had little contact with the Court; she remained unmolested in Athens during the German occupation and, after travelling to London for her son Philip's marriage in 1947, continued to observe strictly her religious vocation. Her brother, Admiral Earl Mountbatten of Burma, served in the Mediterranean from 1948 to 1954 and was a frequent guest at Corfu and Tatoi. But it was in July 1949 that, as his cruiser squadron lay in Navarino Bay, Queen Frederica visited his flagship and slipped into the Admiral's cabin to honour such an entertaining family friend with an apple-pie bed. Next day, to the Queen's chagrin and personal disbelief, an exchange of naval signals let her know that a 'loyal steward' had detected the practical joke before the Admiral went to bed that night.

In the spring of 1954, a year after England's coronation festivities, Queen Frederica found a new and bright focus of attention for the increasing number of journalists for whom the peregrination of royalty made easy writing. She accepted, on free charter, the liner ss *Agamemnon* for the so-called 'Cruise of Kings' through the Greek islands. On this occasion the King and Queen of the Hellenes entertained more than a hundred members of royal families from twenty nationalities. The guests came from everal generations, ranging from Prince George of Greece and his wife Princess Marie Bonaparte – who thought 'the atmosphere anachronistic' – through the age-group of the dowager Queen Helen of Romania and Queen Juliana of the Netherlands to sovereigns of the future, such as the sixteen-year-old Prince Juan Carlos of Spain, who was ten months older than Princess Sophia of Greece. 'It was a tremendous success,' Queen Frederica recalled in her memoirs, 'Not one row, not one single difficult moment during the whole ten days.' The voyage of the *Agamemnon* had an important consequence for the Greek people. There had, as yet, been little tourism in a kingdom internally still disrupted by the devastation of the civil war. Now, as Queen Frederica wrote, 'the shipping companies began to organize cruises exactly following the pro-gramme we had worked out, and soon hotels and other facilities on land also began to bring in the tourists' money'.

After the apparent success of the King and Queen's first state visit to Turkey in June 1952, there followed further journeys abroad which also required the exercise of diplomatic tact: to Belgrade as guests of Marshal Tito and to Rome as guests of the

Aboard ss Agamemnon *during the 'Cruise of Kings', 1954. This was the first gathering of the royal families of Europe since the Second World War.*

Italian President; to West Germany, where the Queen's parents were still living; to the Lebanon and Ethiopia, India and Thailand; and to the United States, where all royal visitors encounter egalitarian republican democrats who simply 'don't like kings'. American support under the Truman Doctrine and the Marshall Plan, together with the military aid which General Van Fleet's mission brought to the armies clearing the kindom of communist rule, had strengthened links between Greece and the United States; and the King and Queen treated both General Marshall and President Eisenhower as personal friends, great soldiers whom they admired and by whom they were held in high esteem. Queen Frederica had developed a keen interest in nuclear physics, and in the United States she was able to visit Chicago University, Oak Ridge and the University of California at Berkeley for conversations with eminent scientists, stimulating her own reflections on the nature of the universe; for the Queen who enjoyed practical jokes was also a deeply serious thinker – 'a fascinating woman', Churchill once observed to Smuts.

In the summer of 1955 it became clear that the head of the Government for the past two and a half years, Field Marshal Papagos, would not live much longer. King Paul held private consultations among contenders for the succession but, after Papagos's death on 4 October, he caused considerable surprise for he chose not a veteran politician, but the Minister of Public Works, Constantine Karamanlis, who –

Ashore at Delphi from the Agamemnon, *1954. King Paul is accompanied by King Michael and Queen Anne of Romania, King Simeon of Bulgaria, the Duchess of Mecklenburg, Duke Louis of Württemberg, Prince Henri of France and Prince Juan Carlos of Spain.*

at forty-eight – became Greece's youngest prime minister. There were complaints of royal favouritism from disappointed politicians, some of whom even said that the King had acted unconstitutionally in not choosing one of their number rather than the lawyer from eastern Macedonia. But both the King and the Queen had been impressed by the vigour with which Karamanlis supervised reconstruction after the earthquakes of 1953–4 and speeded up the modernization of the Piraeus harbour and the main railway link with central Europe. King Paul's choice was far-sighted: for eight years Greece enjoyed an unprecedented stability of government and, for most of those years, industrial development flourished, while the tourist trade rivalled tobacco as a staple industry. At least until 1962 the King and his Prime Minister understood each other well. When, in October 1956, the parliamentary opposition voted against an increase in the King's personal revenue because of the alleged anti-democratic activities of certain courtiers, Karamanlis rallied to the support of the sovereign. Further parliamentary attacks in October 1959 were roundly condemned by the Prime Minister, who asserted that a smear campaign by a number of opposition deputies and journalists was deliberately intended to 'undermine the foundations of the state'.

In his inaugural speech as prime minister Karamanlis told parliament that he saw three tasks ahead of him: to find a solution to the Cyprus question; to modernize the character of public life; and to revitalize the economy. King Paul acknowledged the importance of all three objectives and for seven years worked closely with his Prime Minister. Cyprus – where four-fifths of the population remained Greek in faith, speech and feeling – was a familiar issue to the King. In an interview with the *New York Times* as early as July 1948 he had gone further than the government of the day in pressing for 'the union of Cyprus with the rest of Greece'. On that occasion his Prime Minister felt compelled to explain that, although His Majesty expressed the *will* of the Greek people, the Government had no intention of raising the matter at such a critical moment in Europe's affairs. By 1955, however, Cyprus loomed larger than any other problem in foreign affairs: the emergence of a vigorous campaign for *enosis* (unification) in the island under the leadership of a new and youthful Archbishop, Makarios III, had provoked a violent reaction within Turkey; and in London the succession to the premiership of the ailing and obdurate Anthony Eden held out little promise for the settlement which George V had vainly urged on his ministers forty years before. It is hard to escape the impression that on at least three occasions before Cyprus was first rocked by violence, patient statesmanship by British ministers who understood the deep feelings of the Hellenic peoples might have saved the island from the long agony of a guerrilla conflict and an ugly civil war.

Throughout the late 1950s King Paul showed masterly tact in handling the vexed question. When, in April 1957, Archbishop Makarios was released from British detention in the Seychelles and arrived in Athens as a popular hero, the King entertained him to luncheon and presented him with a high decoration; but, after his momentary gaffe in 1948, no agitation by the Greek Cypriots ever induced King Paul to court popular favour by striking a public attitude over *enosis* which might have embarrassed his ministers' dealings with other governments. Ultimately the cherished hope of welcoming Cyprus into the Hellenic kingdom was denied to King Paul, but he continued to back Karamanlis during the negotiations of 1959–60 which brought into being the independent republic of Cyprus. The King felt constitutionally bound to honour a soldier whom his parliament regarded as a hero and in March 1959 he accordingly conferred on Lieutenant-General Grivas the Medal of Valour and the Grand Cross of the Order of George I. Grivas had risen to prominence during the last years of the resistance to German military occupation. Returning to his native Cyprus in the 1950s, he assumed the military leadership of the Greek-Cypriot guerrilla movement against British occupation. The King's award to Grivas of two distinguished decorations puzzled many in Britain and the United States who, though sympathetic towards *enosis*, remained uneasy at the incursion into politics of a temperamentally volatile army officer with extreme right-wing beliefs. They feared not Grivas, but the principles which he represented.

King Paul also supported Karamanlis in seeking fulfilment of the other two tasks he had set himself in his inaugural address. It was natural that the monarch should wish to see political life purged of scandal and corruption, a constant complaint of junior army officers contemptuous of civilian government. He welcomed, too, the

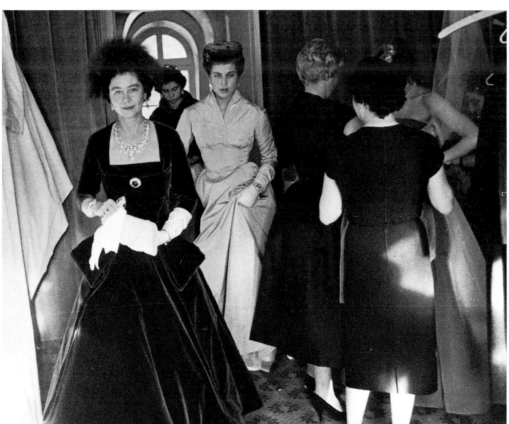

Top *The return of King Otho's regalia to Athens in December 1959. In the speech which King Paul is delivering he praised Otho as 'a Hellene ... who laid the foundations of the Greek State'.*

Above *Queen Frederica and Princess Isabelle of France at Dreux for the wedding of Princess Hélène, 1957.*

gradual change which brought women into political life: not least among the memorable dates of his reign is 29 February 1956, when Lina Tsaldari was sworn in as Minister of Social Welfare, the first woman member of a Greek cabinet (Council of Ministers). King Paul duly carried out all his civic duties conscientiously, rejoicing in what optimists hailed as Greece's 'economic miracle'. Like his predecessors, he inspected troops at distant garrisons and laid the foundation-stones of public buildings, but, just as Queen Frederica continued to take a practical interest in children's communities throughout the kingdom, so the King would associate himself with major industrial projects: thus in July 1957 he was at Ptolemais to open a lignite plant and in November 1958 at Aspropyrgos, near Athens, to mark the completion of the oil refinery there. He inaugurated Greece's first nuclear reactor in August 1961 and, although in poor health, in June 1963 he was at Eleusis for the opening of a steel plant. Yet he remained a critic of many visible changes brought to Greece in the early years of his reign, complaining in particular of the unattractive utilitarian character of so many tourist hotels rushed up in Corfu and other places of quiet, natural beauty. It is largely thanks to King Paul's persistence that Lycabettus, with its white chapel crowning the cone, still stands out unblemished on the Athens skyline, for in January 1961 the King opposed proposals for a funicular railway, unless the aesthetic pleasure of looking up at the hilltop could be safeguarded by concealing such a concession to tourism from the public eye – as, indeed, happened.

Five days before Christmas in 1959, a king of the Hellenes received for the first time a royal crown. When Otho I, King of Greece, was deposed in 1862 he took back with him to his native Bavaria the crown, orb and sceptre he brought to Nauplion in 1833 but with which, as a Roman Catholic in an Orthodox kingdom, he was never invested. Neither George I nor his successors possessed the regalia of kingship: the Greek Orthodox Church has no coronation ritual, and the Office of Crowning is the sacramental part of the marriage service. But in 1959 the head of the Royal House of Wittelsbach, Duke Albrecht of Bavaria, sent his son Prince Maximilian to Athens in order to present his great-great-uncle's regalia to the reigning dynasty. King Paul used the opportunity to speak of the debt of modern Greece – and, in particular, the city of Athens – to the Bavarians, praising King Otho as 'a Hellene ... who laid the foundations of the Greek State'.

Fashions in education had changed since the days when Prince Paul and his sisters travelled to school in Sussex – or, indeed, since the early Thirties, when Princess Frederica led a protest movement against cricket among the girls of North Foreland Lodge. The King himself was founder-chairman of the governors of Anavryta College, a school founded near Kifissia on the principles of service to the community and self-fulfilment under open skies which the renowned educationalist Kurt Hahn had brought to Gordonstoun. Crown Prince Constantine was a pupil at Anavryta for nine years, while his sisters, the Princesses Sophia and Irene, went to Schloss Salem, the original Hahn school in Germany. The Crown Prince's enthusiasm for sailing – which was shared by the family as a whole – led him to take up yacht racing in 1958, and for two years he would sail regularly from Tourkolimano (now Limin Mounikhias)

Top Crown Prince Constantine keeps himself fit and agile during his training. An accomplished sportsman, he won a gold medal for yachting at the Olympic Games in Naples, 1960.

Above A happy husband and father at Marathon: King Paul with Queen Frederica and Princess Sophia.

out into Phaleron Bay, perfecting his Dragon-class sailing technique. Between 29 August and 7 September 1960 he was helmsman of *Nereus* for the seven contests of the sailing Olympics at Naples, with two young companions (Eskitzoglou and Zaimis) as crew and Princess Sophia standing by in reserve. Apart from the final day, the Crown Prince kept *Nereus* among the first four in each race, a consistently good performance which enabled him to become the first Greek since before the First World War to receive an Olympic gold medal. Not surprisingly, he was accorded a civic welcome when he returned to Athens. In that autumn of 1960 there could be no doubt of the widespread popularity of the royal family in general, and the heir to the throne in particular.

Nine months later the Crown Prince and his elder sister were in England for the Duke of Kent's wedding at York Minster. There Princess Sophia met once more Prince Juan Carlos of Spain, who soon afterwards came to spend the summer with the royal family at *Mon Repos* in Corfu. Their engagement was announced in mid-September 1961, with the wedding planned for the following spring. For the sixth time in eighty years the Greek Parliament was asked to approve a dowry for a royal princess and, though the amount was smaller than on earlier occasions, in March 1962 the Opposition fiercely contested the proposal in three days of hot-tempered debate fully reported in the newspapers. The Opposition's tactics, which included a boycott of royal occasions, made no difference to the dowry or the wedding preparations. But thereafter relations between the Palace and Parliament were strained. The first grumbling in the Opposition newspapers coincided with reports of a speech by King Paul to army officers at Salonika in which he declared, 'God has united us! I belong to you and you belong to me.' Normally the King's words would have gone unnoticed; they affirmed no more than the traditional bonds linking a commander-in-chief and his officer corps in common service. But in 1962 the speech evoked a protest from George Papandreou as leader of an Opposition which continued to fear military dictatorship, and the speech left the Prime Minister uneasy at the drift of events.

Princess Sophia's wedding was celebrated happily in Athens on 14 May 1962 with double ceremonies, at the Roman Catholic cathedral in Panepistimiou Street and at the Orthodox cathedral in its square off Ermou Street. More than a hundred royal guests came to Athens, although no longer among them was that venerable giant Prince George; in December 1957 he had been buried at Tatoi. But there were still links with a historic past: the state landau of 1889 trundled out yet again as a bridal coach; and present once more was the bride's grandmother Princess Victoria, Duchess of Brunswick, at whose own wedding in 1913 the rulers of the British, Russian and German Empires met for the last time. There was, too, a portent of the future; for, as Queen Frederica was to record, at the reception after his sister's wedding Crown

Left above At the ceremony to mark Crown Prince Constantine's coming-of-age in 1958, King Paul delivered a carefully-phrased speech on the nature of kingship. Here, after the ceremony, father and son exchange toasts.

Left Crown Prince Constantine comes of age in June 1958 and takes his oath as an officer in the Greek armed forces.

Left *King Paul with Queen Frederica at the court ball to celebrate his 60th birthday.*

Below *King Paul, Queen Frederica and Princess Irene leave the cathedral in Athens on the King's 60th birthday, 14 December 1961.*

Prince Constantine 'would dance only with Anne-Marie', the youngest daughter of his distant kinsman, King Frederick IX of Denmark.

Four months later, when the deputies were faced with fresh proposals to increase the royal revenue, a new bitterness crept into parliamentary attacks on the monarchy. On 3 October Karamanlis sent King Paul a curiously phrased letter which, although emphasizing the King's popularity, listed six points 'insignificant in themselves' which 'could be damaging': complaints of ostentatious living; too frequent visits abroad; royal speeches whose contents were unknown to the Government; royal expenditure requiring additional revenue; absence of a government spokesman at the Palace; failure to have the Queen's Northern Provinces Welfare Fund constituted on a regular legal basis.

This remonstrance, which seemed to put a trusted prime minister of seven years standing among the snipers at the monarchy, produced a long and reasoned reply from the King. He brushed aside Karamanlis's six points easily: the Greek monarchy was less ostentatious than any in the world; journeys abroad were briefer than in earlier reigns, and modern transport made it possible to return speedily home in case of an emergency; speeches on moral, religious or philosophical questions embodied the King's thoughts rather than those of his minister, while as Supreme Commander of the Armed Forces he claimed the right to address the army and navy 'with such words as I think appropriate'; expenditure requiring extra taxation should be avoided, but he pointed out that he economized by travelling about the country by jeep and using a converted minesweeper as a substitute royal yacht; the absence of a government spokesman was not his fault; and, although he agreed that the Queen's Fund should be reconstituted, he resented a campaign of vilification aimed 'not only against my person but also against my wife, my children, and my late parents'. He reproached Karamanlis for not having explained to Greek public opinion the need for increased royal revenue, for failing to protect the royal family by forestalling unjustified attacks in Parliament and the press, and for not giving publicity to royal gestures of goodwill. In this instance he cited the recent donation to the state of his private estate at Polidhendri, east of Larissa for development as an agricultural training college.

The King's letter provided Karamanlis with good ammunition to safeguard the security of the throne. But sniping by Opposition deputies and journalists continued. The Queen was insulted; and, for the first time since his accession, there was a reference to the monarch as 'a foreign King' – a ridiculous epithet to apply to a born Athenian who had fought for Greece in the dark days of 1922 and 1941 and, from long experience, understood the Greek people better than anyone else in his kingdom.

The year 1963 was critical for the Greek monarchy. In March centenary celebrations of the dynasty began, with a state visit from King Frederick and Queen Ingrid of Denmark, on the eve of Independence Day. It was natural for the two old Protecting Powers, France and Great Britain, to have a place, too, in the centenary: no French head of state had ever been the guest of a Greek sovereign; and, quite apart from other considerations, King Paul and Queen Frederica had long wished to make a state visit to London, their hopes persistently frustrated by the twists and turns of

Left *The wedding of Princess Sophia and Prince Juan Carlos in Athens, 14 May 1962.*

Below *The Independence Day parade in Athens, 1963, during the centenary celebrations of the dynasty. King Paul takes the salute with King Frederick IX of Denmark and Crown Prince Constantine beside him. Behind the saluting base is the Ionic portico of the University, completed in Otho's reign.*

the Cyprus problem. On 20 April Queen Frederica and Princess Irene came to England on a ten-day private visit, principally for the wedding of Princess Alexandra of Kent. Outside Claridge's Hotel they were confronted by angry demonstrators seeking a political amnesty and Mrs Betty Ambatielos sought to petition the Queen on behalf of her husband, a communist imprisoned since the civil war. The Queen and her daughter were pursued for about a hundred yards into a cul-de-sac where they found refuge in a small house leased by a visiting American. This frightening experience was exploited by the media; one group of right-wing English newspapers became so outrageously hostile to Queen Frederica personally that Karamanlis urged the cancellation of the projected state visit to Britain later in the summer. The King and Queen did not agree with him, but the matter was still in the balance when President de Gaulle's plane landed at Athens on Monday, 13 May.

On the following Sunday the royal family were entertained at a splendid banquet in the French Embassy. As he was returning home King Paul was taken ill; he was rushed to hospital and underwent an immediate operation for appendicitis. The royal powers thereupon devolved upon Crown Prince Constantine, who acted as President de Gaulle's host on a one-day visit to Salonika, in which the two dignitaries were accompanied by Karamanlis. To Queen Frederica and her son – perhaps to the French President, also – it seemed on this occasion as if Karamanlis was seeking to upstage the sovereign's deputy. Relations with the Prime Minister's office became strained and remained so throughout the royal convalescence.

The King may have suspected that his general health was poorer than his physicians admitted. Yet he was determined to fulfil two engagements dear to his heart: his duties as Europe's only Orthodox ruler led him to visit Mount Athos with the Crown Prince and participate in the ceremonies to mark the millenium of the monastic community (which the Ecumenical Patriarch had postponed for a month because of the King's illness); and, whatever the advice of his Government, he would accompany Queen Frederica to London for he was confident that, in the quiet and patient discussions of family diplomacy, it would be possible to tighten those bonds of Anglo-Greek friendship which media irresponsibility seemed so willing to loosen. To the King's surprise, Karamanlis carried his opposition to the visit so far that on 11 June he resigned office, thus ending the longest term of continuous office for any Greek prime minister.

Political commentators looked for deeper explanations for his fall. Some believed that the economy was unsound. Others said then, and later, that Karamanlis was shaken by the angry attacks of Papandreou's socialists after a car ran down and fatally injured the 'peace march' campaigner Grigorios Lambrakis in Salonika (although judicial enquiries conducted under a later socialist government failed to find political origins in this brutal killing). Nevertheless King Paul issued a long personal statement immediately after Karamanlis's resignation in which he confirmed their 'difference of opinion' over the state visit to London and emphasized his personal desire for a happy relationship with 'the gallant British people' who 'have always come to our side in times of peril'.

President de Gaulle with King Paul at the start of his State Visit to Greece, 13 May 1963. Before the visit was over, King Paul was rushed to hospital to undergo an emergency operation for appendicitis.

King Paul and Queen Frederica were in Britain for only three days, in the second week of July 1963. There were low-key demonstrations – many by nuclear disarmers angered by Greek commitments to NATO – but cheers, too, in the streets of Westminster and the heart of the City. Queen Elizabeth II created King Paul a Knight of the Garter, making him a member of the oldest unbroken order of chivalry, as his brother King George II had been in 1938 and their grandfather before them. The King scored a remarkable personal success, especially when he spoke at the Lord Mayor's luncheon in the Guildhall. But photographs of the visit show a tired man, and an anxious wife. Some weeks after his return to Athens King Paul complained of pains in his legs.

The Queen travelled to Madrid in December for the birth of her first grandchild, Princess Elena. In January 1964 she crossed by sea to New York to receive an honorary degree from Columbia University, while in Greece an election campaign was in full swing. On 2 February a discreetly phrased telephone call from her son brought the Queen hurriedly back by air to Athens. King Paul needed an operation. Yet, although he was in pain, a sense of duty compelled him to put it off until after the general election on Sunday, 16 February (which brought George Papandreou's 'Centre

Crown Prince Constantine and Prince Michael of Greece follow the Ecumenical Patriarch Athenagoras and King Paul at the ceremonies which marked the millenium of the monastic community on Mount Athos in June 1963.

Union' of leftish liberals into office). On Wednesday, 19 February, the new Government came out to Tatoi to take the oath in their sovereign's presence. A five-hour operation for stomach cancer was carried out next day, after the King had signed a decree establishing the regency of Crown Prince Constantine. For a week there seemed some prospect of recovery, but it could not be sustained.

The pages of autobiography in which Queen Frederica left a spiritual record of the last days of her husband's life are deeply moving. In their intensity of feeling they recall the letters of the Queen's great-grandmother which described the battle against cancer of the Emperor Frederick – King Paul's maternal grandfather – in those two tragic weeks at Potsdam sixty-six years before. But, in place of the Lutheran piety of old Prussia, King Paul had around him Greek Orthodoxy's visible pledges of mystic salvation. Once again, as in 1915, the holy ikon of Tinos watched over a royal bedside, a fast destroyer having brought the sacred image to Piraeus, whence the Regent sped it by car twenty miles out to Tatoi. On Thursday, 6 March – so Queen Frederica records – with King Paul's last breath, 'the small flame of the oil lamp' burning before the ikon 'suddenly went out'.

Constantine II takes the oath as King of the Hellenes on the evening of his father's death, 6 March 1964. Behind him are his sister, Crown Princess Irene, and his father's cousin, Prince Michael.

6

'A LEGACY OF GREAT RESPONSIBILITY'

When Crown Prince Constantine celebrated his eighteenth birthday in June 1958 he attained his majority in law. To mark the occasion King Paul held a ceremony in the Parliament Building, the old palace, at which his son took his oath as an officer in each of the Greek armed forces. At the same time King Paul delivered an injunction so solemnly worded that it was to become, in effect, a testament of kingship. He emphasized that the monarchy was rooted not in Divine Right, but in Divine Favour, a gift to be treated as 'an outstanding mark of honour and a legacy of great responsibility'. It was the duty of a sovereign to work indefatigably 'for the advancement and glory of Greece ... uphold steadfastly the democratic principles of our institutions and the constitutional liberties of our people ... be the protector and guardian of our Holy Church', keep the armed forces 'devoted to duty and battleworthy' and be ready to 'redress offence by pardon, discord by unity, error by truth, doubt by faith'. And in a fine phrase, worthy of the noblest of monarchs, the young prince was told he should 'Always remember that it is better for the King to suffer than that suffering should fall on the Nation and the Country'. This advice set King Constantine II a high standard of attainment when, less than six years later, he came to the throne. Though the precepts might be a sure guide to conduct, the moral dilemmas to which they gave rise needed mature judgement if they were to be resolved justly. Was it right, in defence of democratic principles, to risk transgressing the constitution?

At first the young King was spared such harsh decisions. He came to the throne with much goodwill behind him, and it was there in abundance six months later when, on 18 September 1964, he married his beautiful Danish princess, Anne-Marie, in what a veteran journalist was prepared to call the most radiant of Athenian royal weddings. Even the 76-year-old prime minister George Papandreou – an old time republican by conviction – was seen happily arm-in-arm with bride and bridegroom. Unfortunately the kingdom was denied the long period of peaceful adjustment which a faltering economy and a new left-of-centre government demanded. Within weeks

of the royal wedding a fresh crisis in Cyprus brought Greece to the brink of war with Turkey; and thereafter external threats to national security intensified the interdependence of the sovereign and his service chiefs.

On 10 July 1965 Queen Anne-Marie gave birth to a daughter in Corfu; and Princess Alexia became the first member of the royal family born at *Mon Repos* since Prince Philip, now Duke of Edinburgh, in 1921. But the celebrations of this happy occasion were soon overshadowed by political crisis. The Prime Minister's decision to sack the existing Minister of Defence and take over that office himself – together with rumours of *Aspida*, a conspiratorial society of army officers with politically leftish inclinations – had already led to tension between George Papandreou and the King; and on 15 July the Prime Minister resigned office. For two months it proved impossible to find a politician capable of forming a government, and during these (exceedingly hot) weeks there were riotous demonstrations and mass rallies which, with astonishing volatility, became anti-monarchical. The slogans chanted by the window-smashing crowd that surrounded the palace in Athens seemed primarily aimed at Queen Frederica rather than at her son – who, indeed, was keeping within his constitutional rights so long as he was confident of finding a prime minister acceptable to the chamber – but the general mood was ominous and ugly. At last, on 24 September, Stephanos Stephanopoulos won a vote of confidence in parliament and was able to head a coalition which unexpectedly survived for almost eighteen months. But the protracted political crisis provided fuel to the enemies of democracy, both on the left and on the right.

Despite the turmoil in the streets of his capital and the constant threat of attack from Turkey, the King sought to emphasize the international importance of monarchy as a detached institution capable of bridging the gap between opposing political creeds. During the same month that Stephanopoulos formed his government, King Constantine was host to the first congress of space scientists, encouraging American and Soviet astronauts to come together rather than treat each other with suspicion. Unfortunately the press preferred scurrilous tales about the past to prophetic speculation over the race to put a man on the moon and the general public was increasingly disturbed in 1966 by a wave of strikes, which also began to frighten foreign investors. There were persistent rumours of conspiracies and evidence of dangerous plots, including (in September 1966) a plan to assassinate the King's personal military adviser, Colonel Arnaoutis. Constant uproar in the parliamentary chamber and the problems of propping up improvised minority coalition governments led, at the close of the year, to an announcement that elections would be held in May 1967. But five weeks before polling day all democratic rights of expression were stifled by a military *coup d'état* which outraged Greece's allies on both sides of the Atlantic.

The 'Colonels' Coup' in the small hours of Friday, 21 April 1967, was carried out by relatively junior army officers who claimed they were saving their country from

Left above *The funeral service for King Paul in the Metropolitan Cathedral of Athens, March 1964.*
Left *Constantine II and his mother follow the bier of King Paul from the cathedral, March 1964.*

communism. King Constantine, taken by surprise, was anxious to prevent bloodshed and he therefore followed a policy of passive resistance. The spokesman for the conspirators, Brigadier Pattakos, was known to him; his principal confederates, Colonel Papadopoulos and Colonel Makarezos were not. The King refused to broadcast a speech which the conspirators had drafted and he insisted that, if the regime were to be treated as a government, it must have a civilian prime minister: a highly respected lawyer, Constantine Kollias, accepted this invidious post. Although the King, looking grim and angry, agreed to be photographed with the conspirators around him, he would not publicly endorse any of the measures which the Colonels proposed. He was prepared to wait until the folly of their actions totally discredited them before casting them aside.

A month after the coup Queen Anne-Marie gave birth at Tatoi to a son, ensuring that the Kingdom of the Hellenes once more had a crown prince; he was named after King Paul, the grandfather he had never known. In that August King Constantine flew to the United States, to watch the America's Cup races off Newport, Rhode Island. Although he was on a private recreational visit, the King took the opportunity to meet President Johnson and both the Secretary of State, Dean Rusk, and the Secretary of Defense, Robert Macnamara. Naturally the King was guarded in making comments on events in his kingdom which the media might pick up, but he was widely quoted as having said, emphatically, 'This is not my government.'

In November 1967 General Grivas, apparently on his own initiative, mounted a series of attacks on Turkish communities in Cyprus. These raids prompted the Ankara government to concentrate an invasion force less than fifty miles from the island and, at the same time, to put Turkish troops along the frontier with Greece on full alert. International pressure forced the Greek dictatorship to disown Grivas in early December, thereby losing prestige in the homeland. It was at this moment, with the Colonels discredited, that King Constantine made his attempt to dismiss them and restore his kingdom's democratic institutions.

The events of 13–14 December 1967 remain puzzling: the evidence of what happened, what should have happened, and what did not happen is far from complete even now. By tapping telephones and using even older methods of spying, the Colonels must have been well-informed of the King's plans, although chance, too, played into their hands. Basically it appears that King Constantine intended to fly from the Tatoi airfield to Salonika and put himself at the head of the Third Army Corps; mobile columns would then head southwards towards Athens, where it was assumed that public feeling would turn against the Colonels once it was known by broadcasts from the north that they had been formally dismissed. But the war crisis meant that the Third Army Corps was no longer garrisoning Salonika; it had gone forward to protect

Right above Constantine II and his bride, Princess Anne-Marie of Denmark, cheered in the streets of Athens on their wedding day, riding through a festive shower of paper.

Right Guests at the royal wedding in Athens, September 1964. From the left: Prince Louis of Baden; Prince Michael of Kent; Crown Princess Irene of Greece; Charles, Prince of Wales; Archbishop Makarios III, President of Cyprus; Princess Christina of Sweden.

the borderlands with Turkey. Accordingly, on Wednesday, 13 December, the King flew not to Greece's second city, but to Kavalla, a hundred miles closer to the Turkish frontier. Instead of being able to rally the country from Salonika, he was isolated in Kavalla. He had hoped for a swift and bloodless stroke which would right the wrong perpetrated on Greece eight months before. By nightfall on that Wednesday it was clear that only if Greek regiments were to fire on each other could the counter-coup be sustained. So terrible a war of brothers was for King Constantine unthinkable. 'My throne is not worth the price of Greek blood,' he declared, 'I want to build my country, not destroy it.' Early on Thursday morning his aircraft took off from Kavalla for Rome, carrying into exile the King and Queen and their two children, and also Queen Frederica and his sister Princess Irene.

The military triumvirate which now governed Greece would not immediately break with the King: without him they risked international ostracism, and they made it clear that he could come back to Athens, on their terms. An arrogant letter from Papadopoulos in February 1968 received a carefully considered and coolly phrased reply. King Constantine refused to return unless he could exercise the sovereign powers vested in him by the constitution; it was not in his nature to serve as a puppet. Many Greeks of public eminence or social distinction preferred to settle abroad rather than live under so capricious a regime, and the King consulted several of them. Some had left Greece earlier still. Karamanlis retired to Paris in December 1963, before King Constantine's accession; the two men exchanged letters in 1967, between the King's return from the United States and the attempted counter-coup. Five days after his arrival in Rome the King spoke to Karamanlis on the telephone. The ex-premier, however, had ambitions of his own and he treated every approach cautiously, in the following April even declining proposed personal talks in Zurich. During the next five years occasional contacts continued, but the two voluntary exiles never met.

While Queen Frederica and Princess Irene remained in Rome, the King and Queen travelled to England and settled at first in Surrey. The King's head continued to appear on the obverse of Greek coins until 1972 when, as if to threaten deposition, it was replaced by a phoenix, the emblem of the military dictatorship. The Hellenic navy had taken no part in the original coup of April 1967 and remained antipathetic to the mounting personal power of Papadopoulos. In the last week of May 1973 there was a naval mutiny, the captain of the destroyer *Velos* taking his vessel to an Italian port rather than continue to serve the dictatorship. A month previously two newspapers, one in Athens and the other in Salonika, courageously printed an open letter to the Colonels from Karamanlis, breaking a long silence: 'Let the government recall

Right above Orthodox bishops officiating at the wedding of Constantine II and Princess Anne-Marie, 18 September 1964.

Right The christening of Princess Alexia, 1965. From the left: Princess Alice (widow of Prince Andrew); Crown Princess Margrethe of Denmark; Queen Ingrid of Denmark; Princess Benedikte of Denmark; Constantine II; Queen Anne-Marie with Princess Alexia; Queen Frederica; King Frederick IX of Denmark; Prince Michael of Greece; Princess Sophia carrying Princess Cristina; Princess Irene; Marina, Princess Michael of Greece; Prince Juan Carlos with Princess Elena.

the King, who is the symbol of legality, and surrender its position to a strong, experienced government', his biographer quotes Karamanlis's long statement as having said. It was sound advice to offer to any fumbling and demoralized administration.

In alarm, Papadopoulos believed (mistakenly) that a common front of exiled royalists and politicians lay behind the naval mutiny. Hurriedly he determined to assert his own authority and complete the constitutional revolution. On 1 June 1973 the military regime in Athens formally deposed King Constantine and set up a republic, of which Papadopoulos fleetingly became president. Eight weeks later a contrived plebiscite rubber-stamped the passing of the monarchy.

Bloodshed in the streets of Athens – where, in mid-November, tanks were used against a protest by Polytechnic students – was soon to emphasize the moral bankruptcy of the regime. On 25 November Papadopoulos was arrested by his own security chief, Brigadier Ioannidis, who thereafter ruled Greece with an iron hand while using the honest and well-intentioned General Phaidon Gizikis as nominal president. In July 1974 the folly of Ioannidis in encouraging the Greek insurrection against Archbishop Makarios in Cyprus brought down a terrible retribution on that unfortunate island. Once more war between Greece and Turkey seemed imminent, but Ioannidis's nominees were in no position to carry out an effective mobilization. On 24 July Gizikis invited Karamanlis to return from Paris and form a civilian government; the seven-year military dictatorship was over.

King Constantine naturally expected to follow back to Athens a statesman to whom, only fifteen months before, the monarch had stood out as 'the symbol of legality'. Within a week of Karamanlis's return a constitutional decree restored the old form of government – but with a vital amendment: until a plebiscite could be held on the monarchy Greece would remain a republic with President Gizikis as head of state. The King was informed that his return would provoke disturbances during a delicate period of political transition. On 17 November 1974 Karamanlis won a landslide victory in a general election. The plebiscite on the monarchy was scheduled to take place only three weeks after the general election. King Constantine, although still kept in exile, was permitted to make personal appeals in two of the four television broadcasts assigned to the monarchists. Karamanlis, basking in popularity as the saviour of the hour, did not identify himself either for or against the monarchy and he imposed a similar self-denying neutralism on his colleagues in government, although allowing them a free and confidential vote. The odds, however, were stacked heavily against the distant exile: on Sunday, 8 December 1974, in a high turn-out of registered electors, the vote went in favour of the republican experiment by a margin of slightly more than two to one.

Almost a year later – on Saturday, 22 November 1975 – King Constantine's elder sister became Queen Sofia of Spain when her husband was proclaimed King Juan Carlos I after the death of General Franco. At the pontifical High Mass which inaugurated the reign on the following Wednesday, there were many representatives of other European dynasties, prepared to give thanks for the restoration of kingship

Right Queen Anne-Marie with her fourth child, Princess Theodora, in her arms after the baby's baptism in London, 20 October 1983. Prince Nicholas, at fourteen, admires his new sister.

Below The funeral of Queen Frederica at Tatoi, February 1981, a sad occasion upon which Constantine II was allowed to spend a mere five hours in his homeland.

King Constantine II and Queen Anne-Marie in London in 1986 at the christening of their third son, Prince Philip.

in Spain after an absence of forty-four years. Queen Sofia's mother was not, however, present that Wednesday. After completing *A Measure of Understanding* for publication in 1971 Queen Frederica became increasingly interested in Indian philosophy and settled for some years in Madras. Princess Irene, a gifted musician, was able in exile to develop still further her skills as a pianist, while also finding fulfilment of the deep family sense of compassionate service by giving active support to famine relief projects. King Constantine and Queen Anne-Marie made their home in Hampstead, on the northern heights of London: a second son, Prince Nicholas, had been born in Rome in October 1969; a second daughter, Princess Theodora, was born in 1983 and a fifth child, Prince Philip, followed in April 1986. There were at that time 164 living descendants of King George I and Queen Olga, about half of whom were under the age of twenty-five.

From London King Constantine was able to serve on the international Olympic Committee. While keeping in close touch with Greek affairs he abstained from what might have been interpreted as political agitation. On 6 February 1981 Queen Frederica, who had settled in London on returning from Madras, died from a heart-attack while on a visit to Madrid. It was natural that she should have wished for burial beside the husband to whom she had been so loyally devoted. President Karamanlis gave permission for the burial to take place at Tatoi six days after the Queen's death; the exiled royal family might attend the funeral, but King Constantine would not be allowed to spend so much as a single night on Greek soil. 'Fearing that monarchist manifestations could provoke counter-demonstrations and riots', so *The Times* reported, the Greek government threw a protective security ring across the roads around the estate, putting Tatoi (as the paper says) 'out of bounds' to the general public. Even so, many thousands of loyal supporters of the monarchy found their way across the hills to the Paleocastro pinewoods and, at one moment, 'a group of supporters carried the King shoulder high'. Among the family mourners at Tatoi on this moving occasion was Prince Philip, Duke of Edinburgh, a witness to so many changes of dynastic fortune in the land of his birth.

After a mere five wintry hours in Greece, King Constantine returned to London. Politically thereafter throughout the 1980s he was content to keep quiet counsel. Yet, as the decade drew to a close, momentous changes began to shake the fabric of society across eastern Europe from the Baltic to the Balkans. The collapse of one-party rule in Marxist republics might be expected to alert neighbouring states to weaknesses within their own systems, especially in a country which had long prided itself on being a bulwark against communism. It was legitimate to question whether political scandal, governmental instability and a faltering economy made democratic republicanism seem as attractive as during the heady enthusiastic weeks which had followed the Colonels' fall. No one sought a return to military authoritarianism, but did 'democracy under a king' still have something to offer? Continuity, international standing, and by now long experience, perhaps? During his years on the throne King Constantine, like his predecessors, was accustomed to issuing a New Year message. For 1990 he revived the practice, giving an assurance that he 'shared the concern of my compatriots in Greece and throughout the world over what is happening'. The New Year message was no call to revolutionary action; it was an appeal for good sense and calm reflection on the problems of the day. For a resilient dynasty, led by a sovereign of personality and vigour, will never slip silently off the margin of history so long as there remains a challenge to which it may yet provide an answer.

THE ROYAL HOUSE OF GREECE

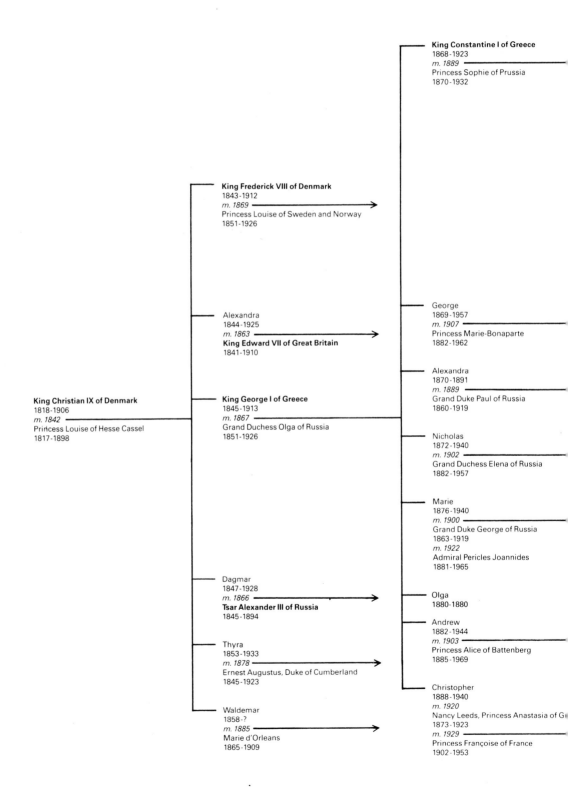

King Christian IX of Denmark
1818-1906
m. 1842 ━━━
Princess Louise of Hesse Cassel
1817-1898

King Frederick VIII of Denmark
1843-1912
m. 1869 ━━━━━━━━━━▶
Princess Louise of Sweden and Norway
1851-1926

Alexandra
1844-1925
m. 1863 ━━━━━━━━━━▶
King Edward VII of Great Britain
1841-1910

King George I of Greece
1845-1913
m. 1867 ━━━
Grand Duchess Olga of Russia
1851-1926

Dagmar
1847-1928
m. 1866 ━━━━━━━━━━▶
Tsar Alexander III of Russia
1845-1894

Thyra
1853-1933
m. 1878 ━━━━━━━━━━▶
Ernest Augustus, Duke of Cumberland
1845-1923

Waldemar
1858-?
m. 1885 ━━━━━━━━━━▶
Marie d'Orleans
1865-1909

King Constantine I of Greece
1868-1923
m. 1889 ━━━
Princess Sophie of Prussia
1870-1932

George
1869-1957
m. 1907 ━━━
Princess Marie-Bonaparte
1882-1962

Alexandra
1870-1891
m. 1889 ━━━
Grand Duke Paul of Russia
1860-1919

Nicholas
1872-1940
m. 1902 ━━━
Grand Duchess Elena of Russia
1882-1957

Marie
1876-1940
m. 1900 ━━━
Grand Duke George of Russia
1863-1919
m. 1922
Admiral Pericles Joannides
1881-1965

Olga
1880-1880

Andrew
1882-1944
m. 1903 ━━━
Princess Alice of Battenberg
1885-1969

Christopher
1888-1940
m. 1920
Nancy Leeds, Princess Anastasia of G
1873-1923
m. 1929 ━━━
Princess Françoise of France
1902-1953

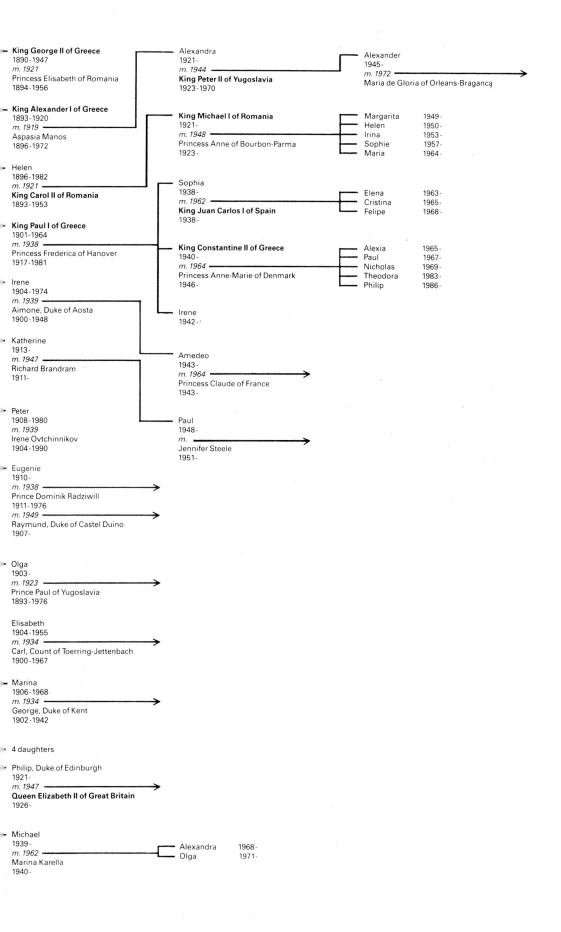

King George II of Greece
1890-1947
m. 1921
Princess Elisabeth of Romania
1894-1956

King Alexander I of Greece
1893-1920
m. 1919
Aspasia Manos
1896-1972

Helen
1896-1982
m. 1921
King Carol II of Romania
1893-1953

King Paul I of Greece
1901-1964
m. 1938
Princess Frederica of Hanover
1917-1981

Irene
1904-1974
m. 1939
Aimone, Duke of Aosta
1900-1948

Katherine
1913-
m. 1947
Richard Brandram
1911-

Peter
1908-1980
m. 1939
Irene Ovtchinnikov
1904-1990

Eugenie
1910-
m. 1938
Prince Dominik Radziwill
1911-1976
m. 1949
Raymund, Duke of Castel Duino
1907-

Olga
1903-
m. 1923
Prince Paul of Yugoslavia
1893-1976

Elisabeth
1904-1955
m. 1934
Carl, Count of Toerring-Jettenbach
1900-1967

Marina
1906-1968
m. 1934
George, Duke of Kent
1902-1942

4 daughters

Philip, Duke of Edinburgh
1921-
m. 1947
Queen Elizabeth II of Great Britain
1926-

Michael
1939-
m. 1962
Marina Karella
1940-

Alexandra
1921-
m. 1944
King Peter II of Yugoslavia
1923-1970

King Michael I of Romania
1921-
m. 1948
Princess Anne of Bourbon-Parma
1923-

Sophia
1938-
m. 1962
King Juan Carlos I of Spain
1938-

King Constantine II of Greece
1940-
m. 1964
Princess Anne-Marie of Denmark
1946-

Irene
1942-

Amedeo
1943-
m. 1964
Princess Claude of France
1943-

Paul
1948-
m.
Jennifer Steele
1951-

Alexander
1945-
m. 1972
Maria de Gloria of Orleans-Bragança

Margarita   1949-
Helen   1950-
Irina   1953-
Sophie   1957-
Maria   1964-

Elena   1963-
Cristina   1965-
Felipe   1968-

Alexia   1965-
Paul   1967-
Nicholas   1969-
Theodora   1983-
Philip   1986-

Alexandra   1968-
Olga   1971-

BIBLIOGRAPHY

In addition to newspapers mentioned in the narrative, use has been made of the following books:

ROYAL MEMOIRS AND LETTERS
Alexandra, Queen of Yugoslavia, *For a King's Love*, Odhams, London, 1956
Andrew, Prince of Greece, *Towards Disaster*, John Murray, London, 1930
Christopher, Prince of Greece, *Memoirs*, Hurst and Blackett, London, 1938
Frederica, Queen of the Hellenes, *A Measure of Understanding*, Macmillan, London, 1971
Frederick, German Empress, *Letters*, ed. Sir F. Ponsonby, Macmillan, London, 1928
    The Empress Frederick Writes to Sophie, Letters 1889–1901, ed. A. S. Gould Lee, Faber and Faber, London, 1955
Nicholas, Prince of Greece, *My Fifty Years*, Hutchinson, London, 1926
    Political Memoirs, Hutchinson, London, 1928
Victoria, Queen-Empress, *Letters 1886–1901*, series 3, vol. 3, ed. G. E. Buckle, John Murray, London, 1932
Viktoria Luise, Duchess of Brunswick, *The Kaiser's Daughter: Memoirs*, W. H. Allen, London, 1977

OTHER BOOKS
The Annual Register of World Events, London, from 1863
Avon, Earl of, *The Eden Memoirs, The Reckoning*, Cassell, London and Houghton Mifflin, Boston, 1965
Bertin, C., *Marie Bonaparte, A Life*, Quartet Books, London, 1983
Burke's Royal Families of the World, vol. I, *Europe*, Burke's Peerage, London, 1977
Campbell, J. and Sherrard, P., *Modern Greece*, Benn, London, 1968
Churchill, Winston S., *The Second World War*, vols. 3 and 6, Cassell, London, 1950 and 1953
Duff, D., *Queen Alexandra*, Collins, London, 1982
Gilbert, M., *Winston S. Churchill*, vol. 3, *The Challenge of War, 1914–1916*, Heinemann, London, 1971
    Winston S. Churchill, vol. 7, *Road to Victory, 1942–1945*, Heinemann, London, 1986
Henderson, M., *Xenia – A Memoir, Greece 1919–1949*, Weidenfeld & Nicolson, London, 1988
Hough, R., *Louis and Victoria, The First Mountbattens*, Hutchinson, London, 1974

Hourmouzios, S., *No Ordinary Crown, King Paul of the Hellenes*, Weidenfeld & Nicolson, London, 1972

Iatrides J. O., *Revolt in Athens, 1944–45*, Princeton University Press, New Jersey, 1972 (ed.) *Ambassador MacVeagh Reports, Greece 1933–1947*, Princeton University Press, New Jersey, 1980

King, J. C., *Generals and Politicians*, Berkeley, California, 1951

Koliopoulos J. S., *Greece and the British Connection, 1935–1941*, OUP, Oxford, 1977

Lee, A. S. Gould, *The Royal House of Greece*, Ward Lock, London, 1948

Lloyd George, D., *War Memoirs*, Nicolson and Watson, London, 1933–6

Macmillan, H., *The Blast of War, 1939–45*, Macmillan, London, and Harper and Row, New York, 1967

Madol, H. R., *King Christian the Ninth*, Collins, London, 1939

Nicolson, H., *King George V*, Constable, London, 1952

Palmer, A., *The Gardeners of Salonika*, Deutsch, London, and Simon and Schuster, New York, 1965

Pope-Hennessy, J., *Queen Mary*, Allen and Unwin, London, 1959

Rose, K., *King George V*, Weidenfeld & Nicolson, London, 1983

Tantzos, G. N., *The Inheritors of Alexander the Great*, Atlantic International Publications, New York, 1986

Woodhouse, C. M., *Apple of Discord*, Hutchinson, London, 1948
Karamanlis, The Restorer of Greek Democracy, OUP, Oxford, 1982
Modern Greece, A Short History, Faber and Faber, London, 1984

Theodoracopulos, T., *The Greek Upheaval*, Stacey International, London, 1976

Ziegler, P., *Mountbatten*, Collins, London, 1985

ACKNOWLEDGEMENTS

Numbers refer to the page on which photographs appear

The illustrations in this book are drawn from the family albums of HRH Prince Michael of Greece, and of Madame John Fruchaud (81, 90), with the exception of the following:

Cecil Beaton/Camera Press London 70; Apesteguy/Gamma/FSP 117 (above); De Keerle/Gamma/FSP 118; The Hulton Picture Company 57, 59 (above right), 87, 88; Mary Evans Picture Library 14 (centre); Mansell Collection 8; Rex Features Limited 117 (below).

Todd Burgermeister kindly photographed the family albums in New York.

INDEX

Page numbers in italics refer to illustrations

125